Quality in the Finance Function

The Financial Skills Series

The rapidly-changing role of the finance function in modern organisations is creating greater and more varied demands upon the skills of everyone involved in the world of finance and accounting. To enable busy professionals to keep up with this pace of change, Kogan Page has joined forces with the Chartered Institute of Management Accountants (CIMA) to create a lively, up-to-the-minute series of books on financial skills.

Highly practical in nature, each book is packed with expert advice and information on a specific financial skill, while the lively style adopted reflects the current dynamism of the discipline.

Already published in the series are:

Cost Control: A Strategic Guide
David Doyle
ISBN 0 7494 1167 8

Quality in the Finance Function
David Lynch
ISBN 0 7494 1145 7

Implementing an Accounting System
A Practical Guide
Revised Edition
Ray Franks
ISBN 0 7494 1052 3

While forthcoming books in the series include:

Strategic Financial Decisions
David Allen
ISBN 0 7494 1147 3

Investment Appraisal
A guide for Managers
Second Edition
Rob Dixon
ISBN 0 7494 1065 5

If you would like to be kept fully informed of new books in the series please contact the Marketing Department at Kogan Page, 120 Pentonville Road, London N1 9JN, *Tel* 071–278 0433, *Fax* 071–837 6348. CIMA members can also contact the Publishing Department at the Institute for further details of the series.

THE CHARTERED
INSTITUTE OF
MANAGEMENT
ACCOUNTANTS
CI*m*A

Quality in the Finance Function

DAVID
LYNCH

KOGAN
PAGE

First published in 1994
Reprinted 1996

Kogan Page Limited
120 Pentonville Road
London N1 9JN

British Library Cataloguing in Publication Data

A CIP record for this book is available from the British Library.

ISBN 0 7494 1145 7

Typeset by Photoprint, Torquay, S. Devon
Printed and bound in Great Britain by
Biddles Ltd, Guildford and King's Lynn

Contents

Preface

The movement of organizations towards quality certification in recent years has developed into a stampede. Many businesses and public sector establishments see BS 5750 as a necessity for their future success and some see total quality management as their preferred route forward. In the rush, the finance function has been largely ignored, on the mistaken premise that accounting already has quality. As a result of quality initiatives in other areas achieving dramatic success, more and more enlightened professionals are realizing that the quality ethic has a greater impact for finance than at first seems likely.

This book is intended to redress the balance of awareness for all finance professionals and for all those who depend upon such experts. The book sets out a framework for understanding the issues and provides an insight into the fundamental concepts. It demonstrates in practical terms how the application of best practice can result in higher standards in finance functions in manufacturing and service industry, and in the public sector. Contributions from a number of senior managers in industry are included in the book, especially in those parts concerned with implementation, so that readers may share their opinions and experiences. The result is a practical guide to assessing and implementing quality in the finance function, with warnings against many potential pitfalls.

During the course of writing the book I received help and advice from people too numerous to list in the acknowledgements, for which I am most grateful. Special thanks are due to Kim Ansell, head of CIMA Publishing, and to Philip Mudd of Kogan Page. To all those who assisted and encouraged me in any way, I extend my heartfelt gratitude.

I hope that readers will gain as much from the reading of this book as I have from the research and writing.

David Lynch
July 1993

Acknowledgements

The list of people to whom I owe a debt of gratitude for assisting me in the preparation of this book is extensive. To the contributors listed below, especial thanks are due for their honesty and openness in allowing their thoughts and opinions to be reproduced and included here:

Amerada Hess
Mr Richard Clout, Finance Manager — Corporate

British Aerospace
Mr Andrew Carr, Head of Management Accounting — SSD

BOC Group
Mr Ian Clubb, Group Financial Director
Mr Bill Connell, Group Controller

Eley
Mr Jim McDonagh, Chief Accountant and Company Secretary

Hoskyns
Mr John French, Senior Finance Manager

Kings Fund
Mr Frank Jackson, Finance Director

Motorola Codex
Mr William Jackson, Director of Finance and Operations

National Grid Company PLC
Mr Dennis Elsey, General Manager Finance
Mr Mike Ormerod, Business Manager — Pennine Area
Mr Graham Bowker, Area Accountant — Pennine Area

National Westminster Insurance Services Ltd
Mr Philip Pierce, Service Quality Manager

Rank Xerox
Ms Myra Johnson, Quality Manager — Finance and Business Process and Information Management

RTM Management Consultants
Mr Robin Tidd, Managing Director

Tesco
Mr Steven Glew, Financial Control Director

Thomas De La Rue
Mr Leslie Cullen, Group Finance Director

1

Financial Problems

QUALITY — AN ENEMY OR A FRIEND?

The culture of institutionalized accounting qualifications has historically lent an air of robustness, dependability and competence to the practice of accountancy of every type and variety. Notoriously difficult examinations have made entry to the profession more and more difficult. Graduates make up an ever-increasing proportion of the student body. The demand for accountants is still buoyant — starting salaries continue to be higher for accountants than for almost any other profession. Policies, procedures and attitudes have been enshrined in statements of standard accounting practice, exposure drafts and other professional agreements (national and international). This is one way in which gentle improvement continues.

On the surface, the finance profession has few real foes, is adequately regulated and provides a useful service to clients, management and other users. Self-regulation on the whole seems to be working and the training for accountants is very well respected. Everything in the garden seems to be sweet-smelling and rosy.

To numerous onlookers, the accountancy institutes are now in a similar position to the engineering institutes in the 1960s, with a near monopoly supply of skills to the market place, good average salaries and 'fat-cat' mentalities.

In the 1950s the Japanese learned how to improve their manufacturing processes. In the 1960s and 1970s they changed the rules of success. Success came to depend upon providing customers with what they wanted. The Japanese became good at fulfilling the needs and wants of their customers, and in the late 1970s and early 1980s they really started to improve.

The engineering professions have since borne the brunt of the dramatic global changes to the unwritten rules of competition and commercial success. British, European and American engineering companies have been decimated. The western mentality, which concentrated on volume and over-engineered products, ceased to be successful. Engineering had become an end in itself, and companies were not sufficiently concerned with adding value for their customers. Customers chose to buy from Japan, where products were cheaper, quicker to obtain and frequently worked better.

Within finance, large mainframe computers met the huge demands for information with flexibility and ease of access. More recently micro-computers have begun to perform the same role even better. Finance professionals should draw elementary conclusions from the experiences of the last 20 years in engineering and avoid apathy and complacency.

The Japanese 'happened' to the engineers; computers are now 'happening' to accountants.

The number of senior managers who consult their finance department before making routine decisions is decreasing. The so-called 'PC power users' and other users of financial information are now able to manipulate data for themselves on their desktop or laptop PC. The fundamental need to ask for information from an accounting department is decreasing, and the need for an ability to 'number crunch' has almost completely disappeared from the profession.

The knowledge that the financial specialist or accountant has 'got the numbers right' is no longer sufficient. There must be certainty that the right questions have been asked and the right options considered. The providers of financial information and services must add value to the organization and be able to prove their added value. Competence must be both apparent and provable.

These changes might be seen as an insurmountable threat to the profession, but a better way of viewing the situation is to see the many opportunities offered and seize the future to achieve even greater potential.

In an American survey, the biggest single reason for the failure of quality improvement programmes was 'the finance department' and there is much to suggest that the UK experience is no different from that of the US. The most important cause of this hostile attitude is an innate antagonism of accountants to quality improvement programmes; this antagonism is probably rooted in the belief that because professional training is so difficult 'accountants always get it right' and therefore do not need a quality improvement programme.

This is the kind of attitude that the engineers used to have.

The engineers learned that this attitude was fundamentally flawed, and they changed. Finance personnel could learn from the engineers that the only sensible response for the professional of the future is the adoption of quality as the way forward to improvement.

Quality in finance is a very personal matter. It is not a procedural problem that a new quality department can come and sort out. Quality is about the way that every accountant and member of the finance function behaves, reacts and performs his or her work in the department.

Just as Deming was misunderstood by the production and manufacturing managers in the US in the 1950s, so the quality message has been misunderstood by the majority of accountants throughout the world. Fortunately, it is not too late for them to change.

How did we get here?

During the traumatic changes to manufacturing industry and the service and public sectors in the last 30 years, many finance functions fulfilled the primary roles of 'bean counter' and 'provider of information'. This made the duties of most internal departments relatively simple; volume was more important than anything else. More data and more financial services were demanded, regardless of whether they were necessary. Employees were conditioned to provide only standard responses; anything unusual or abnormal could not be accommodated. Reports were all standard and different information was neither available nor requested.

At a higher level, the finances of all businesses were treated similarly and directly compared, whether they were involved in apple trading or growing oranges. Progressively less and less detailed financial information was used to make decisions, and ratios and their derivatives superseded genuine industrial knowledge.

This has led to two problems:

1. High-level generalizations lead to poor financial decisions.
    Some UK conglomerate companies have been under-performing for a number of years. Some of them have collapsed, possibly due to the lack of detailed knowledge of business needs.
    Financial results from a company drilling oil wells cannot easily be compared with the results of a clothing manufac-turing company. Diverse needs, and disproportionate invest-ment requirements, may lead senior management to take compromise rather than optimal decisions.
2. Low-level demands for very detailed data and statistics.
    Junior managers who require detailed analysis have frequently been last in line for good information. Histori-cally, finance functions solved the problem of being unable to provide data by giving managers the audit trail prints and telling them to find the information for themselves.

The underlying reason for both of these problems is that the information and service provided by the finance function has in the past been seriously flawed.

Inflexible attitudes

Henry Ford once declared that his company would supply cars in any colour, so long as it was black. A similar inflexible and regimented attitude is prevalent in many finance functions. To take just three examples:

1. Many organizations are unable to provide information users with simple volume statistics on the same report as financial numbers.
2. Others compare capital investment opportunities of assets providing definite cash returns with those where zero cash is returned.
3. Some companies pay no attention to business requirements and only look at whether the projected financial return is adequate to meet profitability targets.

Flawed decision-making usually occurs when an organization is asked to choose between an investment opportunity that would definitely improve the quality of the product or service, and an investment that may improve profitability. In the vast majority of companies, insufficient information is produced to make an informed decision, with the result that the finance function is allowed to suggest that a probable profit is a better choice than a quality improvement.

On another level, in backward-looking organizations the primary motive for the existence of the finance department was negative — accountants were the checkers of the accuracy and honesty of other staff; they 'blew the whistle' and advised the implementation of tough decisions.

During the 1960s and 1970s the culture of many western organizations that were founded on highly technical knowledge treated finance as a black art. Consequently, very few financially-qualified personnel ran either large state enterprises or large private industrial or service companies.

In the late 1970s and the 1980s finance rocketed to importance as business realized that finance was just another commodity. New management styles were introduced and asset stripping was replaced by 'leveraged buyouts', management buy outs (MBOs) and management buy ins (MBIs). The manipulation of numbers became an art form, and books were published showing how even the largest companies engaged in question-able accounting practices. A new breed of financial services mega-traders was created — professional brokers who were paid handsomely to trade the dubious paper documentation of dubious companies in dubious markets.

In an environment where city analysts were paid more than many of the finance directors of large PLCs, the mayhem that was largely created by the requirement for more and more unnecess-ary data was hardly surprising. As pressure grew from external stakeholders for more data, and internal users clamoured for ever more detailed data, the finance function lost sight of its reason for existence.

Quantity versus quality

From the end of the Second World War, organizations throughout the world were exhorted to 'do more'. Industry and agriculture developed their attitudes, processes and measures in response to the idea that efficiency was the most important criterion for management. 'Pile it high' mentalities pervaded companies from stock management through to credit control. Volume, volume and volume seemed to be the three rules for success in international trade. Effectiveness did not matter.

In the 1970s the volume world began to disintegrate. Customers no longer wanted a single choice of a commodity good. Discerning purchasers wanted their personal preferences catered for, and at a very competitive price. This new-found consumer choice had been created by companies responding to demand stimuli: Toyota could build a car in Japan (to customer specifications) within four hours of receiving the order in the United States; Rank Xerox found that their competitors' UK selling price was lower than their own ex-factory costs.

The minute attention to detail of Japanese manufacturers when they were engineering and developing their products provided both reliable and cheap manufacturing; this led in turn to swift and massive marketing success. Where perceptions could be positively affected, Japanese effort was focused on exceeding customer expectations. For example, Nissan cars were fitted with radios and heated rear windows as standard years before their European counterparts. Failures were less frequent in Japanese products than in UK manufactured goods, so imports from Japan gradually came to be recognized as quality products.

By the early 1980s UK, US and European industry was on the defensive — their products were not what the customer wanted, at a price they wanted to pay. Worse still, in comparison to imports, UK manufactured products were frequently inferior. Any reputation for quality was waning fast. While the government concentrated attention on the growth of service industries, the balance of payments in manufacturing became a constant problem. More than 20 years too late, industry woke up and began to look for the reasons why the Japanese had become so successful.

By adopting the techniques, attitudes and methods of quality, the Japanese had shown the world that more products could be produced from fewer resources, at less cost, with less effort, and provide greater profits.

The Japanese have shown the world that quality was, is, and shall be, more important than volume, and that volume is not a limiting factor to quality. They have shown that by following academic instruction closely, business success can be achieved by meeting customer needs with higher quality, higher volumes, and lower real prices.

CREATING SUCCESS

A review of the causes of Japanese success reveals that they employed just a few key points. They were simply:

1. Understand your own business.
2. Discover the customers' needs and wants.
3. Satisfy the customers' needs and wants.
4. Make constant improvements.
5. Empower staff to take personal responsibility and action.

A cliché was coined for the new sales environment in which customers' needs were recognized as paramount — quality.

The Japanese learned quality principles from Dr Deming, Professor Taguchi and others during the 1950s and 1960s. Adopting the quality techniques and changing the culture and philosophy of large companies took them many years, but they persevered and have benefited from higher productivity, lower unit production costs and faster development times. This has led to consequent improvements in employment, balance of payments, and infrastructure investment.

In the early 1970s a few American organizations took on the tenets of quality and started to improve. During the 1980s the pursuit of 'excellence' became a buzz word, but industry still failed to satisfy customers. When management generally realized how far behind international competition they had fallen, important steps were made to redress the growing international imbalance and new initiatives were started. In 1987 the US Senate established the Baldridge prize to recognize quality in US industry. The reaction in Britain and Europe has been slow, but in the late 1980s and in the 1990s industry has begun to pick up on quality initiatives, and the level of enthusiasm for quality appears to be gathering pace.

All of this has applied to production, processing and manufacturing — now the same principles must be applied to overhead functions, the key to which is the finance function. Accountants are no longer needed to number crunch basic data and create and rework huge cash flows on endless analysis paper, because computers perform these tasks more accurately and reliably than humans. Information users are now used to having large volumes of data available, and they demand more than just data. Financial skills are now required by all levels of management within the organization to provide and interpret information, not just by the board.

FINANCE FUNCTIONS AND FINANCIAL SERVICES — THE DIFFERENCES AND SIMILARITIES

The finance function consists of two distinct occupations:

Group 1. **Internal function**

The internal finance function provides both financial information and financial services.

Financial information This includes providing facts and figures that range from capital investment advice and forecasting, to budget preparation and the analysis of recent results and statistics.

Financial services These include the credit control and accounts payable functions, self-insurance and internal audit departments.

Group 2. **External function — financial services**

These are provided by external companies and include bank and building society services, insurance companies, loan agencies, brokers and financial consultants. Some financial services can be the providers of financial information.

In government statistics, all employment within internal finance functions is included in the sector to which the services are provided. External financial services outlined in group 2 above are counted separately as the financial services sector.

Though the two are treated differently for statistical purposes they have many similarities, being two sides of the same coin. The internal side represents the services provided to the buyers and sellers in transactions; it treats money as a medium of exchange by which measurement is possible. The external side simply treats the medium of exchange as another commodity that is capable itself of being bought and sold.

Below are examples:

☐ Group 1: create accruals to provide against bad debts.
   Group 2: create a system of insuring against bad debts, charging a percentage to users for every cheque cleared through the system. This is not factoring.
☐ Group 1: raise sales invoices and chase overdue payments.
   Group 2: recover debts — factoring.
☐ Group 1: analyze risk to decide whether to invest or not.
   Group 2: analyze risk and calculate that claims will be less than the total fees charged to those that wish to avoid risk — insurance.
☐ Group 1: make sales overseas and recover money in foreign currency.
   Group 2: for a percentage, will risk that the future exchange rate will not change, and provide currency now in exchange for currency later — foreign exchange cover.

☐ Group 1: borrow money at fixed or floating interest rates.
 Group 2: lend money to higher-risk companies at fixed or floating rates with money borrowed from lower-risk companies — lending.

☐ Group 1: provide information to external users.
 Group 2: estimate whether the value of the company will increase or decrease based upon latest information, and buy or sell stocks accordingly — Stock Exchange.

☐ Group 1: will assist internal management to make decisions.
 Group 2: assist management and individuals to improve the performance of their savings and/or investments — consultancy.

☐ Group 1: produce reports and monitor the trading of international commodities in international markets, completed by traders.
 Group 2: trade and speculate on the reaction of governments to changes in the balances of trade between countries, expressed as changes to interest rates — money market.

☐ Group 1: running routine data collection functions, and producing timely management information in the required format.
 Group 2: exactly the same as for group 1 — facilities management.

For all of the financial functions within an organization, an alternative financial service exists that could perform the same role as its internal service. Over recent years major competitors have developed to the internal finance function operations of companies and organizations. The central government thrust towards market testing for local authorities and state enterprises has pressed its own staff into competition with facilities management companies. Partly as a consequence of these moves, large and efficient providers of services have been created, and these are being further developed to compete in broader sectors.

The primary difference between the internal and external sectors is that recognition of actual customers and users tends to be poor in the former. This commonly results in a failure to identify critical success factors, and so ensures that the finance function is internally focused; external users are often ignored and receive a correspondingly poor service. External users of information and services, such as suppliers, customers and bankers to the organization, rarely complain of receiving a poor standard of information. They believe that the internal management within the organization receives an equally poor service.

Financial services companies have usually identified their customers clearly, and understand what must be achieved to maintain their rates of success. They attempt to show potential new clients that by using their available services, client targets and objectives will be met quicker and better than would be otherwise possible.

The growth of the financial services industry

During the 1980s the image of finance was transformed from a backroom operation controlled by merchant bankers into a retail operation in which whole new types of products became available. The range of financial products and instruments readily available to companies became immense, ranging from normal finance leases to off balance sheet funding, the buying and selling of options, and the swapping of tranches of loans and their repayment schedules. Personal finance has also progressed; individuals may now contract out of the state pension scheme; taxation avoidance packages and measures have become tradeable commodities; and many insurance and endowment policies now have a second-hand value. Pensions have developed to the stage where loans can be made against a pension taken as security.

Over the last ten years the services sector of the employment market has grown with remarkable vigour (see Figure 1.1). In every advanced country in the world financial services plays an essential role within the overall service sector (see Figure 1.2), and in the G7 countries total overall growth in services is accounted for by the growth in financial services. More than two out of three of those in work in the advanced countries of the world are employed in the service sector (see Figure 1.3).

The growth of the financial services sector has been especially noticeable in the UK, where in 1980 the sector employed approximately 7 per cent of the working population; by 1990 the comparative figure was over 11 per cent. Between 1981 and 1991, employment in the UK in financial services grew by almost 1.0m. Over the 20 years since 1971 high growth rates have more than doubled the numbers employed in the industry to over 2.6m people. The financial services sector can be said to have caused the boom years in the mid and late 1980s (see Figures 1.1–1.4).

Financial services employment consists of three main groupings:

1. Banking and finance;
2. Insurance and pensions;
3. Other.

The numbers employed in the financial services sector peaked in 1991, when employment in the banking sector stalled after 15 years of strong growth. Employment in the insurance sector slowly increased for over ten years, and stopped in 1991. In the 1980s the main growth sector was 'other', but this expansion

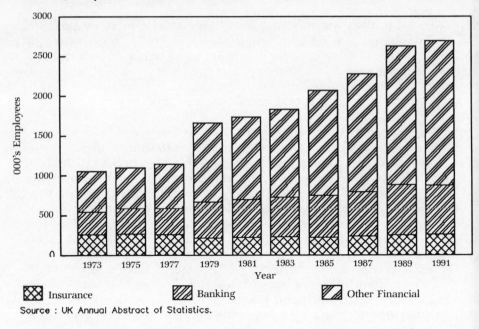

Source : UK Annual Abstract of Statistics.

Figure 1.1   UK growth of employment in the financial services sector

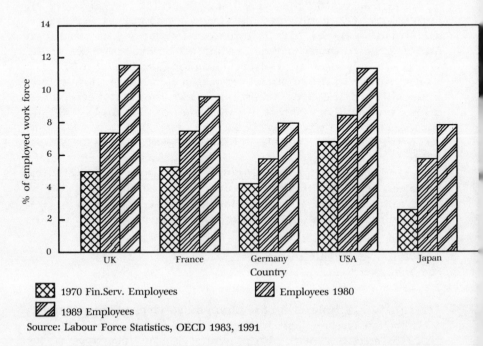

Source: Labour Force Statistics, OECD 1983, 1991

Figure 1.2   International growth of employment in financial services over
20 years

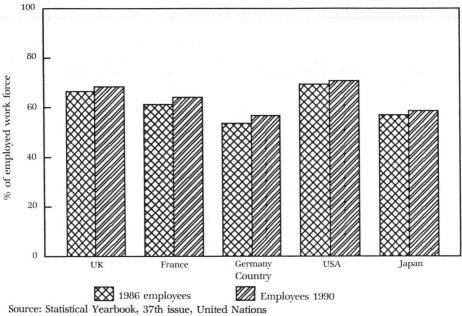

Figure 1.3 International comparison of employment in service industries

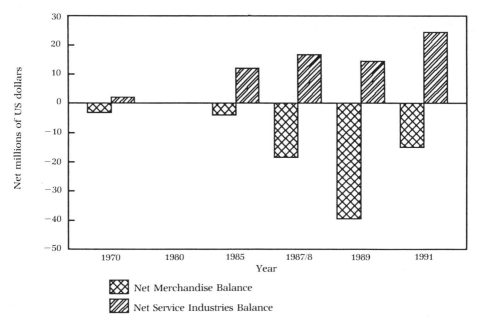

Source: Statistical Yearbook, United Nations 1991, and UK government statistics

Figure 1.4 Balance of payments extract

slowed to almost zero by 1991. Professional business services statistics are reported in the 'other' sector, which includes professional accountancy and financial consultancy services, making up approximately 60 per cent of the sector total.

Implications for slower growth within the sector

If the slow-down of growth of employment and overseas earnings suggests that the market has reached a level of maturity, three implications result:

1. The customer will recognize the oversupply of financial services, and become very much more selective of suppliers. Purchasers will become price sensitive. This will result in the financial collapse of some smaller operations that fail to address the needs of their customers fully.

    In mid-1993, the announcement was made that all parties to financial services transactions to individuals must declare their commissions before the transaction is completed. This supports the suggestion of the market maturing, as regulators on behalf of customers become price sensitive.
2. Employment opportunities will decrease as efficiency and effectiveness increases in those companies that positively seek improvement. The total number of employed financial specialists will therefore decline.
3. In an increasingly buyers' market, faster and more user-specific expert advice and assistance will be demanded by the users of information.

    To meet the demands of an increasing diversification of need, financial skills will continue to be required to construct and develop services.

    Rather than an ability to add and subtract, initiative and creativity will be required to identify the means to satisfy customers' needs better.

The role of the finance professional is central to the continued success of the financial services industry, to generate and re-engineer products and services, and to maintain those products and improve services after sales have been completed.

International aspects

International competition is likely to increase in importance as trade barriers between European countries are gradually removed. This pattern will extend slowly so that financial services and their products are transportable both within the European Community and throughout the world. This internationalization has already occurred in the major markets for financial instruments — stocks and shares, bonds, and money.

In a mature market, the degree of international competition is likely to become more intense. Other countries will improve by importing developed skills from countries like the UK; they will improve the techniques for themselves and re-export them back to the UK. This process has happened with many UK industries, from shipping and clothing, to cameras and cars.

As European and East European countries import financial skills to learn and assimilate techniques, they will develop and improve methods and products for themselves. New financial methods, systems and products will be created all over the world in response to market demands.

A CHANGE OF DIRECTION

The stock market crash of 1987 wiped out much of the demand for impressive financial abilities in the top management of many organizations. The perception that organizations could best be run by those who 'understood the numbers' had generated enormous expectations of profits and fantastic earnings opportunities for a select few. The one-third reduction in average stock market values brought the concepts of leveraged buy outs crashing to a halt under the weight of the enormous scale of corporate borrowing. The crash also brought the exploration for new financial markets to an abrupt halt. The impact on older financial services markets was severe, and thousands of workers were laid off in the City of London and the South East.

During the ensuing recession, companies rediscovered that finance was only one of the ingredients in a successful business, and they re-learned that financial success was more dependent upon the underlying business than upon the ability to manipulate statistics and numbers. City observers blamed the crash on shareholders' demand for:

1. increasing short-term company profits;
2. growth to provide constantly improving dividend yields;
3. capital growth of share values.

Prior to October 1987 the atmosphere of increasing share values had encouraged growth by acquisition funded by borrowing. Companies often purchased growth by taking the target's forecast of future earnings, applying discount factors for risk and interest, and if the resulting number was less than the company's own price/earnings ratio, the deal would go ahead. 'Short termism' was a result of too much concentration on the financial numbers of organizations rather than the underlying business. Since 1987 many more examples of business failures illustrate the neglect of the underlying business parameters in the quest for growth, eg Ferranti, BCCI, Maxwell, Polly Peck, Heron, Coloroll.

The quality revolution has moved the goal posts dramatically for every kind of organization. There has been a shift away from providing 'just another' item, to always selling and servicing 'the perfect one'. Volume and the financial numbers are not so much the god of profit and cash flow as they were; the satisfaction of customers' needs and wants has returned to the top of the corporate agenda.

The answer to business difficulties was a move away from financial generalization and concentration on the numbers towards recognizing the customer. As an indication of this, a small number of finance functions have made a tremendous effort to try to find out who their users are. This is because there is more to the word 'customer' for finance than for any other department or section. Finance should never see its customers as being merely the person that asked for information; customers are any stakeholders with an interest in the organization.

As a direct result of too narrow a definition of the concept of customer satisfaction, finance has been unnecessarily constrained. Where finance defines its customers as only being those that routinely ask for or receive service, over 80 per cent of the true customers are excluded. Many more people use the information produced by the department than ask for it (eg staff requesting pay rises, based on increased company profits; or predators assessing a company prior to making a bid).

Both the concepts of customers and customer satisfaction must be explored further, because every stakeholder may be seeking the fulfilment of completely different objectives, yet be using finance functions in similar ways.

CREATING A VALUE

A new dawn is being forced on the financial specialists because they are beginning to realize that the specialist skills and services which they offer to the rest of the organization only have value if the recipient of the service perceives a value. If the recipients are unable to see where value has been added by the skill of the specialist, they will solve their own problems and satisfy their needs in other ways. Where the application of financial skill could have added substantial value, the failure to use the skills will result in a proportionate increase in cost or losses. In some instances organizations could collapse as a result.

To address this potential for major error within a corporation, those within it must recognize who the other stakeholders are, and their relative importance to the organization, and they must comprehend the crucial role of finance in satisfying both internal and external stakeholder needs. Such an understanding will be achieved when finance personnel really start to take account of their customers and users, and adjust their behaviour accordingly.

The lack of recognition of the skills of the finance function staff is generally caused by fear and misunderstanding on the part of the users. Fear can originate from the abuse of power by finance staff if, when requested to help justify or to authorize some expenditure, they always say 'No'. Misunderstandings have arisen because non-financial staff have not been encouraged to understand finance jargon, and in many cases have themselves avoided involvement in the figures and information produced.

A significant proportion of UK management and staff see accountants as a necessary evil, appreciating financial skills only because accounts have to be audited each year. Substantial numbers of organizations, both large and small, produce financial information which is not used in their decision-making processes. In these situations, the finance functions concerned are singularly failing in their obligations to employers, stakeholders, and the rest of the profession by not getting the message across properly.

As an example of potential misunderstanding that can arise:

A subsidiary of a large company closed its three remote administrative functions in late 1991, saving a total of approximately £240,000. The finance staff in their new central roles refused to allow outlying offices to have word processors and facsimile machines, on the basis that all services were provided centrally and available for all to use.

The staff at outlying offices ceased to write letters to customers and suppliers, as they could not get typing done quickly enough. Foremen spent up to 50 per cent of their time driving between sites to pass time sheet and job information to one another that could not wait two days for the internal mail system.

Following the introduction of facsimile machines, word processors and printers, at a cost of less than £20,000, the company calculated that the saving of wasted man-hours was in the order of £180,000 per year.

Where the opinion of financial specialists is not valued, users of information will do without such opinions, leading to significantly increased risks for their organizations. When finance personnel do not spend sufficient time with new users of information, the quality of decision-making will rapidly decline and the whole organization will suffer.

The finance function, both internal and external, must create a value in the eyes of their users — the consequence of failure is commercial disaster.

2

Quality Levels

REASONS FOR ADOPTING QUALITY

Dramatic change in the structure of industrial employment has always caused disturbance and unrest. The technological revolution that has been underway for some years is now forcing professionals to ask important questions concerning their finance functions. The main question is 'Why does this department exist?'

There are distinct parallels between the present situation for finance functions and a number of historical examples of dramatic change in the structure of industrial employment. By comparing these examples and learning from how the problems were resolved, lessons may be applied to today's predicament.

1. The Industrial Revolution created massive new employment in the cities, which resulted in fewer people working on the land. The market structure for manufactured products changed completely. Products that were previously hand-made and extremely expensive were made instead by machine and modestly priced. Demand increased massively, and employment was created in new industries.

2. The quality revolution initiated by Japan in the 1960s has led to new levels of productivity. Fewer people now work in manufacturing organizations. Manufacturing emphasis has changed from being volume driven to being uniqueness driven — in which products may be built for one specific customer. As manufacturing employment declined, so new markets were created in financial services and employment transferred to meet the demand.

3. The technological revolution, which has also been running since the 1960s, has led to huge amounts of data being made available, increased the ease of electronic communication, and speeded up response times. The creation of information has changed from being highly labour intensive to being highly computerized. Manufacturing and service industries have been equally affected by the new communication possibilities, new computational powers, and the ingenuity of computer software products. Significant numbers of

people are now employed in the software and networking markets.

The lessons to learn from these observations are straightforward:

☐ As one industry declines, another grows.
☐ As more users receive an improving service, the efficiency of that service increases.

Both of these factors result from the progression of society from the old to the new, and provide an illustration of industrial life cycles and their consequent employment structures. Technology is making the transition from the old to the new faster than expected and perhaps in a less ordered manner. Whereas skills and technologies used to last a lifetime, skills acquired now may only last half a lifetime.

In most medium-sized and large organizations, middle management is a buffer between the directors and the workers in the company. On the basis that the cost incurred does not add sufficient value to the goods or services produced, this whole tier of middle management has been systematically removed by many companies. Since 1985 many thousands of middle managers have been made redundant by utility companies such as BT and others. This removal of the senior and professional tiers is the practical result of the industry restructuring its employment through applying quality techniques. The finance profession must now apply the same principles to itself.

WHAT IF QUALITY IS INTRODUCED INTO FINANCE?

Over recent years quality attitudes have changed the nature of retailing, manufacturing and services, and major improvements have been made as a result. The concept of manufacturing *after* an order has been taken and delivering the goods within one week was unthinkable until quality attitudes and technology made it possible. Motor vehicle manufacturers are capable of doing this, numerous computer printer manufacturers achieve such a turnaround, and supermarkets turn their stocks over within one week.

An opportunity now presents itself to the finance departments of every organization to change the way that financial functions are performed. This opportunity means changing the way accountants and financial experts think, modifying the way in which tasks are performed and completed, and desiring continuous change within the finance function. Why plan to achieve something in a twelve-month period when it could be completed within one month? Why budget?

The reasons to make changes are simple:

☐ to increase revenue;
☐ to decrease costs;

☐ to make greater returns on capital;
☐ to survive longer than the competition.

The practical changes that will be made are specific to each organization, as they will depend upon that organization's needs. Computers already supply the technology for change, responsible managers and financial necessity provide the stimulus, and finance personnel can provide the results.

Many recognized levels of quality exist, ranging from the very basic (most of the British Standards) to the internationally renowned (world class manufacturers). Companies and organizations should decide the level that they wish to aim for, and plan to make achievement practical. The benefits that will flow from such initiatives depend on the level and scale of commitment to quality concepts; they normally range from 1–2 per cent to over 70 per cent improvement in overall performance. The higher the initial benefit, the more likely the benefit is a one-off, but this should not be assumed in every case. Mould-breaking improvements occur in industry more and more frequently, and if the organization sets out to encourage them, even more will be achieved.

As a result of introducing quality into finance, major improvements will include the following:

1. Basic data will improve, leading to a better understanding of the business and the real recognition of the customers for financial information.
2. From discovering customer needs and wants, greater value will be added to the whole decision-making process, so ensuring the continuing and improving success of the organization.
3. Improvement of total satisfaction for all levels of customer will lead the organization to optimize its development and meet stakeholder requirements.
4. Utilizing feedback to make continuous improvement will result in the improvement of revenues, the reduction of costs, and better utilization of resources.
5. Empowerment will result in improved motivation, morale and job satisfaction. Efficiency and effectiveness will subsequently improve.
6. Financial functions will be seen to provide value-for-money services, by increasing speed of response while improving the volume and relevance of information.

Some organizations set themselves targets when adopting quality initiatives, such as:

☐ Halve the staff.
☐ Halve the time taken.
☐ Double the accuracy.
☐ Double the use of the product/service.

The Japanese have shown the manufacturing world that high quality can also mean greater volume. The finance function and accounting professionals can show their organizations that where information is available that meets user and stakeholder needs, better decision-making will follow.

In the same way that modern world class manufacturing techniques have transferred emphasis away from product volume to customer satisfaction, world class accounting can transfer the professional accounting emphasis away from data and information generation to the improvement of decision-making in the organization.

THE ASCENT OF QUALITY

Most new organizations that start out in business try to meet their customer needs and improve their own financial performance. As they grow, methods to implement improvement and systems to facilitate and recognize achievement are developed. Where quality is understood to be a component that can be added to the product, real quality in the organization does not exist. Real quality is integral and indivisible. Achieving this in finance leads to less waste of time and effort, greater concentration on the core business services and products, and improving financial performance.

To help individuals and organizations recognize whether they have quality within their culture, a framework has been developed that incorporates recognized milestones and targets on the way to achieving a quality finance function. As shown in Figure 2.1, five primary stages have been identified as being the equivalent of steps on the stairway toward quality.

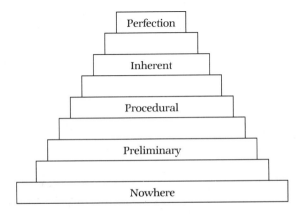

Figure 2.1 The stairway to quality

The quality ladder is a framework for understanding the overall achievement of the whole organization. Every organization has a relative positioning on this quality ladder; even the worst organizations try to achieve something and can be recognized in the framework.

Even though the lowest of the identified stages is titled 'nowhere', this does not mean that there is no quality. It represents the point at which quality systems can be said to have started. In reality, the lowest point is where the organization is off the map; here, there is no conception of how quality can have a positive impact. Both large and small organizations can fall into this category.

Identifiable characteristics are shown below.

Being nowhere

At this level, the only systems in place are those of 'good management'.

'Good managers' tell staff how to work, decide routine priorities, intervene whenever a difficult or unusual decision is made, and constantly fail to delegate work to their subordinates. The individuals concerned are unable to see that their actions lead to a perpetual dependence upon their personal intervention, which is a major limiting factor to the overall performance and capacity of the whole group.

As a result of poor organization and delegation, no one has enough time to communicate with one another or with the customers/users, and everyone waits to be told what to do.

Personal loyalty to 'the boss' and a feeling of camaraderie are common among the staff. There is little understanding of loyalty to customers.

While the management and staff of the whole organization have the best intentions, constant apologies have to be made to customers for failing to meet expectations and promises.

Staff are not highly motivated, and morale is often low. Even senior staff are rarely trusted to make a decision of any sort. Everyone tries to 'do their best', but it is never good enough.

The top management know and understand the mission and objectives of the organization, as they have spent at least one weekend locked away in a hotel with a consultant discussing the publication of their new mission statements. The different statements have been circulated, but they do not appear to relate to the tasks of the organization and so few employees understand them. There is a lot of managerial frustration that staff 'simply don't understand why we're here'.

Financial information

For finance departments that are 'nowhere', the majority of output is actually scrapped — in that it has to be re-worked, or dumped, or is not used by the recipient.

Reports are produced, but distribution is limited to the boss, unless staff side-step the system. The majority of information is transmitted through the grapevine.

Most of the reports provide enormous lists of data which is personally reviewed and highlighted by the boss for investigation by the staff. Unless a query is picked up at this review stage, it is missed completely.

Standard financial reporting can be monthly, but is normally less frequent. Special reports usually fail to provide information on which decisions can be made, as it is either out of date by the time it is available, inaccurate, or contains insufficient detail.

Financial services

The purchase ledger is run on the whim of the boss, and the resulting antagonistic and offensive phone calls from suppliers cause continual problems.

The credit control section is known for its uncompromising approach to late payers. Substantial legal costs are incurred annually, and the bad debt write off amount is always larger than the previous year.

Wages calculations are nearly always perfect, but extreme problems occur when someone tries to make a change to the system. Changes are generally not allowed. The sales commissions systems are always a source of argument and frustration.

Preliminary quality

Management thinking in these organizations has advanced to the stage where staff are trusted to fulfil their primary functions and roles. This is because the managers and staff recognized that improvement was possible, even though everyone may be doing their best. The first elementary steps were taken when staff were shown how to think about their work content, and management encouraged personal responsibility for change rather than chastising attempts at change.

Communication within and between the ranks of staff starts to engender a mutual understanding of contributions to the total effort.

Training for specific requirements and for the attainment of specific skills is frequently undertaken. Clearly defined job descriptions, and a strict hierarchy of superiority among staff are hallmarks of this preliminary level. The directors' canteen and toilet facilities are a source of amusement among staff, and more attention is paid to the trappings of position than to the content and result of endeavour.

Throughout the organization, managers and staff are oriented very much on the task, not the personal contribution. Because all attention is focused on the practical tasks that are performed, the development and evolution of strategies is unknown. Where there is a high degree of stability, the resulting lack of visionary capabilities rarely causes short-term problems.

Some advanced managers have introduced standards and procedures for their own departments, but the rest of the organization spends most of its time fire-fighting.

Financial Information

Scrap in finance is visible in piles of computer print-outs on the floor and on shelves, or in stacks of files ranked in priority order on the floor of a large office.

'Information' is original data reformatted into huge computer print-outs that are impossible to pick up with one hand. Exception reporting is unknown.

Reports are only produced in standard formats — to get anything else takes weeks, and uses highly expensive programming time.

Everything is fully costed, with values attached to products and services for local overheads, divisional overheads and corporate overheads where applicable. Substantial amounts of time are wasted in deciding whether the allocation of cost is fair and reasonable.

Profit/cost centre reporting is common at this level, and major arguments are caused by the system of recharging between departments. The system of allocating head office costs causes more friction and discussion than poor performance at operational level.

Financial services

The purchase ledger staff have a routine schedule that usually pays suppliers approximately two weeks late, except at Christmas, when everyone is paid three or four weeks late because it happens to coincide with the year end and the financial director wants to publish final accounts with as low a bank overdraft as possible.

Credit control have started to listen to the customers, and carry the messages into the organization. Some minor changes have been made, but they have had little effect.

The wages department is subcontracted to an outside company, and payroll information is a closely guarded secret. Even so, everyone knows what everyone else earns.

Budgets rule all expenditure. If the amount was not budgeted, it is usually a waste of effort to seek approval for any spend other than essential unforeseen repairs.

Procedural quality

Once communication has started and staff, managers and directors can understand one another, staff can be encouraged to recognize that some tasks have similar inputs, employ similar methodologies in the transformation or creation process, or have similar outputs. To minimize duplication, and maximize efficiency, procedures are written to ensure that staff perform their processes in a predefined fashion to a pre-set, consistent level of quality. Staff rarely understand the difference between efficiency and effectiveness.

Large organizations can administer a bureaucratic system in which tasks tend to be repetitious, since most of the required outcomes can be described as standard outputs. Indeed, large organizations positively encourage a bureaucracy, because measurement of documented achievement is very much simpler than measuring a perception or an individual service.

Procedures also provide benefits, in that staff responses can be conditioned and 'brain-washed' in. During the 1980s the North American response 'Have a nice day' became the butt of many jokes, but when used properly it can help customer perceptions. Many of the procedural responses generate positive interpretation from the customers — the chef walking round the restaurant, asking if the meal is enjoyable; hotel receptionists asking whether the stay was enjoyable; cashiers inviting the customer to return in the future.

With proper training to operate the procedures and attain the specified standards of delivery, staff may deal with customers and provide far better levels of satisfaction than previously possible.

As staff learn to conform to new quality expectations, the managers learn to delegate some of their responsibility. When expectations are not met, blame is apportioned among the vulnerable staff, which makes the environment more fearful than necessary.

Staff have an understanding of their role within their own function, but do not understand the whole company. This often causes inter-departmental political fights about which of the high-flying trainees and which of the dodos are allocated to particular departments.

Procedural changes are discouraged, as flexibility was not built into the original system. Over a period of time the rigidity of procedures actively limit and constrain satisfactory performance. This rigidity ensures that continuous improvement is prohibited and the company then fails to meet its customers' changing needs.

Many organizations become disillusioned with quality at this level, as there is a lot of quality talk, but little quality action. In reality very little additional work is required to further transform attitudes and thus become an organization with 'inherent' quality.

Many departments and organizations have painstakingly built up sets of procedures that apply to the various tasks undertaken by staff. Unfortunately, their efforts have been rendered irrelevant as the staff have not been inspired by quality or converted to its principles. Before procedures can affect an organization, the earlier stages of quality must be successfully completed — they are like gates that can not be jumped over or avoided.

Financial information

Scrap is measured as a percentage of the total output. In finance there is no scrap percentage because reports are hidden in large cabinets, occasionally used, then dumped.

Everyone can show you the procedures manual, but no one uses them. Quality is commonly understood to exist, purely on the basis that everyone is highly paid, highly qualified, and highly respected.

Senior managers have instituted a 'clear desk' policy, under whose rules all desks must be cleared every night before leaving — whether work is continuing or not. There is little control over whether tasks have been fully completed, resulting in finance staff running many tasks simultaneously, with few ever reaching a satisfactory conclusion in time.

Most users have stopped asking for information or action from the department, as the historical answer has always been 'No'.

Most of the managers have got their own PCs with the result that they only ask finance for information when the request has become unavoidable.

Financial services

Both purchase ledger and sales ledgers are run according to strict rules. Customers are not allowed to make late payment unless acting under court instructions following bankruptcy proceedings. Everything is produced according to standards, and if the recipient does not like it, nothing can be done anyway.

The constrained attitude towards providing services caused users to find ways of working to bypass the normal systems — agreeing prompt payment terms with preferred suppliers and ignoring demands for payments from others until receipt of court warning letters.

Inherent quality

This level describes those organizations whose philosophy has passed beyond procedural and bureaucratic quality, and which believe that the behaviour and attitude of staff are more important than the task they perform.

Responses of the staff are conditional upon customer need, and are not 'conditioned' by procedural response. The response to a question to which the employee cannot provide a solution is 'I know someone who can'.

This kind of organization avoids problems in the first place by operating good planning systems, to which the staff willingly work, and by empowering the staff to provide personal and individual solutions.

Staff are frequently trained beyond the normal expectation for their particular job. Specific vocational training, such as behavioural and awareness training, plays an equally important role alongside non-vocational training, such as languages, pottery, art, etc.

Individuals understand both their own role in their section and the role of the section in the overall organization. Directors and management have a broad vision of where the organization is heading and how it will get there. The staff understand and concur with the steps that will be taken to achieve the aims, and in many cases the staff themselves decide upon the action that will be taken.

The fluctuating needs of the market represent an opportunity to the organization and internal structures change frequently to accommodate new requirements.

The staff pride themselves on offering a range of solutions from which customers can choose the one that fits their needs most adequately.

Customers enjoy dealing with these kinds of organization — the staff are helpful and the products always meet expectations.

Financial information

On the rare occasions when scrap is found, it is measured in parts per thousand or per million.

A large proportion of finance function staff time is spent with line managers and staff, at their location, helping to define and specify information reports that are required to help make various business and operational decisions.

Very rarely is information late or action forgotten. When it is, no one is sacked or carpeted; action is taken to ensure that the problem does not recur.

Financial services

The credit control function attempts to help solve problems for customers and takes the attitude of 'How can we help you to pay the bill?' A sale is only complete when payment has been made by the customer, and something was learned from the process.

The purchase ledger arranges for payment to be made on due dates — whether an invoice is received or not. The well-being of the supplier is seen as essential to the well-being of the organization itself.

Wages are fully automated, and little is secret between employees. Everyone knows that some individuals contribute greater added value to the organization than others, and reward is consistent with contribution.

Perfection

One can imagine a situation where an organization can identify and plan to provide for all of its customers' needs and wants, and then operate to meet those needs, on time, every time.

This organization would require limitless funds to pay for the ultimate in flexibility of product and service, and limitless time in which to plan and create all of the potential outcomes.

On a very limited scale, airlines attempt to provide this to users of their first-class service.

Financial information

Anything and everything is produced just when it is required, in the required format, on time, and complete. There are no errors or omissions, and prefect accuracy and all of the associated data that is required is available.

Financial services

No sooner does the user or customer recognize a need than the service is available. This would entail the ideal, tailored for individual needs, exactly matching user requirements.

Even though 'perfection' can never be achieved, in certain circumstances it can be worth aiming for.

GETTING TO THE QUALITY LEVEL YOU WANT

When starting a quality initiative, the extent of change desired should be assessed in relation to the starting position of the organization. This will enable the accumulation and application of appropriate resources, and the appropriate timing and emphasis will result in the most suitable changes being implemented within the organization.

Quality within a large organization can develop at different speeds in the different functions and affect the overall attainment of improvement. The levels of achievement throughout the organization generally relate to technical delivery competence, which can be recognized through kite-marks and awards. Finance function quality relates to intellectual skills and ability transfer and deployment, which has very different measures. However, a matrix can be created to illustrate how these phenomena interrelate. This is discussed later in this book.

Managers of the finance function must decide on the level of quality that is most appropriate to their own needs and demands, as each level has an associated investment requirement. If a quality project is starved of resources, positive achievement may be at risk. Prudence is a sensible approach to adopt. The steps to take are as follows:

1 Recognition

The organization must recognize its current circumstances and the gap between current and desired perceptions. This realization must be based in fact and not in hope.

Many companies have developed substantial quality initiatives but then failed to consolidate the learning processes among staff and senior management. This was because they did not recognize the extent of problems, or where the learning had to be effective. Unless the foundations of quality are solid and reliable, the potential benefits will never be wholly realized.

2 Planning the conversion

The steps required to convert the organization from its current position to the desired position must be taken incrementally.

The steps can only be taken as quickly as the slowest stakeholder groups permit — many initiatives have failed from attempting to do too much too quickly.

Develop strategies to engender the right attitudes and beliefs simultaneously, and then communicate the messages.

3 Action

Changes planned and communicated to staff must be acted upon to show commitment and to maintain momentum. Monitoring systems have to be in place and operating adequately to provide feedback on the degree of success or failure achieved in the programme. Sufficient flexibility must be incorporated to account for unexpected eventualities, and adequate resources and time allowed to plan and perform the required actions.

4 Maintain

Keeping up to the standards and targets that the organization has set for itself will not be easy. New employees must be brought up to the desired level of understanding for their role. New methodologies must be communicated to all of the staff to keep them abreast of developments and expectations. Benchmarking comparison with external parties must be made routinely to ensure that the change within the organization is progressing at least as fast as that of the competitors.

STOP PREPARING USELESS INFORMATION — START SUPPORTING DECISIONS

The role of finance has always been to educate and inform all the stakeholders that have an interest in the decision-making process. Until computers replaced the manual collection of data, most of the time within financial functions was spent gathering basic data. Precious little time was spent on widening and improving the role of interpreter and communicator of information.

The need to perform mundane tasks has gone. Report writers, automatic DCF calculations, executive information systems, fully integrated ledgers, module based packages — all are direct substitutes for finance department labour. Powerful computers and user-friendly software has taken over most of the mundane data collection and report generation that was once performed by finance personnel. The only reason that finance staff continue to write anything by hand is personal preference.

The habitual collection, presentation and re-presentation of data has blossomed from extended use of computers. Many financial information departments collect and create useless information that will not be used to add value for the organization. More time is wasted on showing numbers in different ways than was ever thinkable without computers, all of which fails to aid the user.

As more junior management staff are empowered to make decisions, the finance function is needed to provide higher standards of support at lower levels of management.

A finance function of quality facilitates and supports decision-making in the organization by providing good basic data and by ensuring that collated data is converted into genuine information. It also applies skill and expertise to problems to ensure that the surrounding environmental knowledge is as complete as possible. Where finance personnel help to create parameters, interpret information and improve the decision-making environment, decision support is a part of normal daily routine. Decision support is the use of skill and expertise to ensure that the best solution for the organization is found, agreed and enacted.

The financial function is the only department in which staff are trained to create, report and interpret financial and non-financial statistics for others. Finance functions should re-focus their efforts on supporting decisions to ensure that the balance of financial justification and organizational short-, medium- and long-term objectives continue to be met.

SLOW PROGRESS

For over ten years the quality of goods and services has been improving substantially across the world as a result of quality and other initiatives undertaken by multinational companies. In spite of the visible improvement that has resulted from these initiatives, the finance function has generally not adopted the principles openly and fully.

A small number of forward-thinking financial experts are taking their organizations into the future by applying quality principles, and are now beginning to reap the benefits after years of toil. Their organizations are lean in terms of employees, powerful in terms of financial strength, and intelligent in how they use information and make decisions. In spite of a significant increase in the number of accountants over recent years and an increase in the relative importance of management accountants, the number of these progressive companies is very few.

Progress towards quality in the financial industry as a whole seems to be moving at a slower pace than in manufacturing. There are fewer articles or books to lead quality thinking for services than there are for manufacturing.

The lack of speed in addressing quality within the finance function is caused by four problems:

1.   Business emphasis on customer-related 'front-room' problems.
2.   Public lack of concern with supporting 'back-room' operations.
3.   The complacency of financial professionals.
4.   Financial institutional interests taking precedence over financial industry considerations, eg pension advice.

Progress has been made, in spite of a large and unwieldy finance industry structure. The main items of progress include:

☐   The professional accountancy institutes are making attempts to consolidate professional qualifications.
☐   CIMA has made real progress in broadening the syllabus for new students to ensure that general management skills are understood and used by the qualified accountant, in addition to financial and numeric abilities.
☐   Forward thinking individuals are introducing the concepts of quality to a wider finance audience, eg BOC Group PLC.

From such small beginnings great potential quality improvement can be achieved, if the major hurdles to progress can be overcome. Some of these obstacles are as follows:

☐   Customers are unable to differentiate between the different types of financial specialists available, eg tax planning, business forecasting, auditing, operational improvement.
☐   The lack of financial facilities is the single most important reason why businesses fail. Businesses and the general public

equate financial experts with the ability to source or with-draw funding.
☐ The profession is believed to be responsible for 'driving forwards while looking out of the back window'.
☐ Regulation of financial advice has not been particularly successful for consumers. There is no regulation of financial advice provided for business use.
☐ In a survey conducted in 1993, the reputation of the accounting profession was very low in comparison to most other professions. Finance ranked below all other pro-fessionals, including solicitors.

Satisfactory solutions to many of these problems will result from the adoption of quality principles throughout the profession. For those that ignore the quality drive, their finance functions will add little or no value to the decision-making process and will disappear, to be replaced by 'palmtop' computers.

Finance functions of quality will survive and prosper because they will positively add value. Their customers will have both reliable data and quality information — because the right questions were asked in the first place. Consequently, the right organizational and commercial decisions will be made. Their managers will be able to plan for contingencies and opportuni-ties knowing that the finance staff can learn from the past and look forwards as well as sideways.

The challenge of the next decade and beyond is for finance functions to contribute positively to their organizations in a far more effective manner, with increasingly fewer resources and with increasingly faster response times. Using a quality approach, this is eminently achievable.

Quality is not the enemy of accounting professionals, it is an ally.

THE CHANGING ROLE OF FINANCIAL FUNCTIONS

For too long the finance function has been the equivalent of the 'gaoler' — refusing requests, keeping information to itself, and taking the view that if the numbers are right then nothing can be wrong. Computing power has turned these arguments upside down because the users of information can gain access to data at almost any time. In a world where information is power, the finance function has to learn to address the change and help users to use the information to wield that power.

Computers have shown financial information users how to produce information for themselves. The rules for the generation, manipulation and use of data have been rewritten and the attitude of the gaoler will not survive in this technological revolution. When customers can help themselves, the financial service provider has to find a new role.

For financial services customers, oversupply is creating a buyers' market and margins are shrinking. The users' greater knowledge of products and services makes customer satisfaction increasingly difficult to achieve.

In many successful organizations, finance has become a facilitator to the organization, allowing a better and faster drive to excellence, and leading to the attainment of the objectives of the organization. The change from a controlling to a facilitating role demands much more attention than it receives because it represents a sea change in attitude for most of those involved in the profession. The intellectual volte-face from being the corporate judge, jury and nursemaid to becoming diplomat, statesman and mentor will be extremely difficult for those that seek to make the important transformation. Changing one's attitude and becoming a team player requires a clear under-standing of the concept that the other team players are themselves customers.

The finance function must attend to the implications of statistics and information and interpret them for users. Positive suggestion must replace critical comment and cynical deeds must be replaced by constructive action. The role of finance in the future will be one of the creation of an environment in which better decisions are possible, wherever that decision is made.

$$\boxed{3}$$

What is Quality?

THE CONCEPT OF TOTAL SATISFACTION

The degree of satisfaction felt by a user or customer that results from the delivery of a good or service depends on two variables:

1. the customer;
2. the good or service.

Although this is extremely simplistic, these variables are the crucial factors that workers easily overlook when they are seeking to speed up a service or merely finish a piece of work. For the finance function the customer may never be seen, spoken to or directly provided with any service. The concept of a tangible customer is therefore misleading and a wider definition is required. The criteria that help to define customers for finance are:

☐   the type of services provided;
☐   the range of users.

In addition to the problem of user identification, the content of goods or services must be carefully defined because finance does not offer a product that can be measured easily against single expectations. Products and services range from basic lists of data, through collecting debts based on reports produced, to trading in complex financial instruments that pass rights to income streams between parties.

The two axes of user and composition of service can be applied to define total satisfaction for the organization. Total satisfaction is:

> Where services are provided to all of the users such that all of the needs of all of the users are thoroughly fulfilled.

This definition ensures that both breadth and depth of analysis and assessment are an integral part of the service provision. Breadth results from the assessment of all of the users — from suppliers and internal users, to external customers and stake-holders. Depth arises from considering the basis of data, its presentation, use and application. These issues are discussed in more detail below.

DETAILING THE COMPOSITION OF SERVICE

The formula that defines the service provided by a finance function has two main aspects:

1. *Delivery* The manner in which the service is performed, involving inter-personal skills, the immediate effect of the provision, and the ambience.
2. *Content* The availability of equipment, intellect or knowledge or benefit provided are the essence of the service event. Also relevant to the content are considerations such as timeliness, consistency and presentation.

Included within content are underlying assumptions. In most organizations, the underlying attitudes and beliefs are embedded within information and services and remain unseen until too late.

Delivery

Many organizations fail to recognize the importance of the service delivery aspects of internal departments to the rest of the company. The manner in which finance function personnel conduct themselves can have devastating effects on the overall efficiency and effectiveness of the organization.

The physical delivery of goods or services to a consumer is the subject of many books concerned with human interactions. In a retail environment the parallel subject is called 'merchandising'. However, there is no comparable name for the one-to-one delivery process for services. For the sake of convenience, in this book we will refer to this as the 'ambience' of the provision of service.

Ambience is itself composed of:

1. the attitudes and style of the providing personnel — listening, thinking, being helpful;
2. the location or channels of the service provision;
3. the pre-dispositions of recipients.

Attitudes and style of providers

Providing personnel is the most significant component of the ambience. They must listen to users' needs so that feedback can be pursued properly, and they must think about their responses and consider any action to be taken. An unhelpful provider of a specialist service can negate enormous amounts of positive work in a few seconds.

Location/channels

The route through which users and customers receive the service should be reviewed regularly. As requirements change and systems develop, new opportunities arise that should be taken advantage of. Direct contact through telephone conversation is a channel frequently overlooked, but many large financial institutions make investment decisions based on services provided over the phone.

Other channels such as third-party comments, advertising media, marketing, sales promotions and public relations initiatives are important. Financial services using these different channels have seen dramatic growth in recent years as a consequence of matching their services to the channel and maximizing all possible benefits (eg, Direct Line Insurance).

Information user expectations can be influenced to some degree by the choice of location for the provision of services. For many financial services, the location at which service is provided is the working location of the recipient. Some organizations use electronic mail to distribute automatically the crucial data from reports, in advance of (or instead of) hard copy print-outs of the information.

Pre-disposition of recipients

Normally recipients know that they will receive service or information, before it happens. They have expectations based on past performance and perceptions of their needs. Two aspects of user disposition are important:

☐ the user's degree of confidence in the service;
☐ the extent of conflict expected to arise from the service.

Confidence is generated from consistently good past performance that, with the benefit of hindsight, has shown the service to be accurate, complete and timely. High levels of confidence tend to diminish the likelihood of conflict.

Conflict arises most commonly from the interpretation of the information, and the emphasis placed on aspects that may be uncomfortable for the user. Where conflict has become a normal part of operation within the organization, an atmosphere usually exists in which trust cannot be created. Significant attention must be paid to the development of an atmosphere in which participants do not fear the exposure of errors within their control.

Content

The content of information can be described at six levels:

Data   Accuracy, consistency and completeness.
Presentation   Timely, relevant, attractive, useful and understandable.
Environment   The surrounding or associated background information.

Action	Being the immediate effect of the use of infor-mation.
Result	The assessment of the results of actions taken by the user, seen with hindsight. Review of the provider, and the efficiency and effectiveness of the service provision.
Assumptions	Underlying information services are both hid-den and visible assumptions. Each should be described to ensure that fundamental flaws are discovered early in the delivery process.

1   Data level

At the lowest level, financial information and services must be:

☐   error free;
☐   consistently collected;
☐   complete.

2   Considering presentation

Poorly presented work can destroy meaning for users just as much as if inadequate data were originally collected. If the message from the information is unclear, the resultant decisions are likely to be incorrect and the organization will suffer.

In outline the main points to remember are:

☐   Present what was required or specified and ensure that the right person(s) actually receives the result of the work.
☐   The abilities of the users should be recognized in the level of complexity and detail that is produced for them.
☐   All of the content should be useful.
☐   Exclude irrelevant or erroneous data that may mislead or divert attention.
☐   Present information in clear formats using descriptions that will be recognized and terminology that will be under-stood.
☐   Where the information or service is one of a series, there should have been recent improvement resulting from feed-back.
☐   Information must be supportable to make further analysis possible.

3   Broadening the environment

Checking that financial information is fully provided and has encompassed adequate data to account for 95 per cent of contingencies can be an extensive process. Likewise, the creation of the environment for financial services can be fraught with problems.

Examples of this are clearly demonstrated by the reams of

paperwork that are completed by personal financial advisers to show that they have done their job adequately.

Some environmental considerations are more crucial than others and depend upon individual circumstances. Routine checks should be a part of the operations within the finance function.

Below are listed the main items that might be checked:

- □ Dates, and the related timing of events.
- □ Scale and scope of the information or service.
- □ Planning, timetable, practicality, and realism.
- □ Infrastructure availability.
- □ Relevance and validity of components.
- □ Potential outcome-influencing factors.
- □ Alternatives to proposals.
- □ Opportunities arising from potential choices.
- □ Knock-on effects, and implications of making choices.
- □ Simultaneous or parallel initiatives.
- □ Relationships between data, events and decisions.
- □ The balance of resources, expertise and emphasis.
- □ Risk analysis — business, financial, personal.
- □ Historical trends, and likely probabilities.

4 Actions to be taken

The application of information or financial service results in action, either to do something or not. If action does result it must be monitored, as must the immediate result of the action. Examples might be whether operational change resulted from the monthly publication of income and expenditure statements, or whether plans are changed resulting from new business forecasts prepared by the management.

Knowing that all of the planning was successful at the right time, in the right place, and for the right people is essential.

Useful information includes:

- □ Did the information or service result in the recipient taking the action that they had expected or desired when specifying the service?
- □ Immediate feedback of perceptions of the entire performance.

5 Result and analysis

Hindsight provides a great opportunity for learning. When more time is available there is less pressure for urgency, and alternatives may be compared and contrasted. When one knows the detailed results of a service, changes can be specified and modelled to suggest the best ways forward.

There is a cautionary comment, however: hindsight is only useful if the learning is applied.

Post-completion analysis is the point at which feedback is formalized into ideas and suggestions for improvement. Assessment may be made against each of the headings: data, presentation, environment and action.

Each of the components may be improved to provide a better or more complete service. Modifications can be made that will enable users meet their objectives more closely.

As a result of later analysis, individual performance is reviewed so that better accomplishment may be recognized and repeated across the organization.

Any unexpected effects of actions on other criteria should be searched for, so that previously unrecognized relationships are discovered.

6 Underlying assumptions

Underlying many sets of data and services are whole series of assumptions that define and constrain performance. These range from time constraints to borrowing limits, and from interest rates to earnings capacity.

Assumptions are usually considered to be secondary to the result, though they are integral to the whole structure of the service. Finance function personnel are normally charged with the maintenance of data integrity.

Underlying assumptions can be more important than data, because they are usually hidden. Inaccuracy within the assumptions will render the whole of the information useless, so it is more important to ensure assumptions are correct before performing any calculations.

Within basic data, errors rarely cause discrepancies of greater than one order of magnitude. Where assumptions are in error, discrepancies are rarely of less than one order of magnitude.

The most frequent assumptions that are later found to be inaccurate include:

☐ timing;
☐ residual values;
☐ costs;
☐ rate of depreciation and interest;
☐ sales volumes and values;
☐ worked efficiency.

For many assumptions, users are the best (and sometimes the only) source of information. Efforts must therefore be made to obtain clear statements from users, defining the assumptions and the conditions under which they may change.

As a last resort, financial opinion alone could specify assumptions but they should be vigorously tested.

Professional assumptions can be among the most unrealistic when reviewed with the benefit of hindsight, eg straight line depreciation.

IDENTIFYING THE USERS OF FINANCE

The point of view of a user of information will always affect how knowledge is used in practice. The best method of transmitting new knowledge will therefore differ between each group of user. For this reason, users of finance function information or services may be grouped by their likely focus of needs. A preliminary framework that addresses the primary points of influence for finance functions is shown below in Figure 3.1.

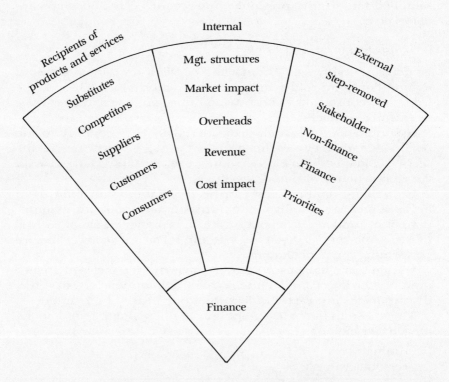

Figure 3.1   Finance fan of influence

The Fan of influence starts to analyze where the finance function may add value within the overall sphere of operation. The three sections take a typical approach to the financial role using internal, external, and products and services as headings. This model should be used to help staff to understand the primary groupings in which influence may be exercised, so that more detailed analysis may then follow. These groups are based upon the users' common needs for information:

☐   Recipients of services: selling prices, procurement, comparisons, alternatives.

□ Internal: cost and organizational structures, cost cutting, costing, efficiency.
□ External: forecasts, budgets, financial reporting.

User grouping

By concentrating on the users' focus of attention, a common approach to the main groups of stakeholder in an organization may be made. Developed from the concepts in the fan of influence, eight sub-groups can be identified:

□ *Recipients*: customers and consumers of the organization;
□ *Internal*: sales (including marketing), operations and support services;
□ *External*: staff, onlookers and suppliers.

These classifications will allow more attention to be paid to individual group needs, so that communication can be designed to meet user needs more closely. As a result of planning how needs may be met with greater clarity and awareness, resources may be closely targeted to meet those needs better and faster.

Recipients

External to the organization are the customers of the organization, who may be separated into two classes:

1. *Consumers*: those that finally use and receive the full value of the good or service, eg the child that eats the sweets.
2. *Customers*: those that decide to purchase, and usually pay for the product, eg the parents that pay for the sweets for the child.

For some, there is no difference between these two categories; for others, making this split positively assists in targeting and defining the environment to be created for both parties by finance. For the finance function, recognition of this position helps to define the extent of additional communication necessary — when resource is scarce, the customers are more important than the consumers.

Internal

Internal users can be simplistically reduced to three groups for these purposes:

3. *Sales and marketing*: have the closest contact with customers, and create and identify needs to specify and deliver goods and services.
4. *Operations*: the creators of the service or good, or those who source goods/services to match the specification.
5. *Support services*: all of the infrastructure that ensures the smooth functioning of both the sales and marketing, and operational departments.

Although organizations generally consist of more actual departments, the above groups describe the generic types of department using their likely information needs as parameters. Each of these main categories has its own service requirements from the finance function.

External

The last main category is that of 'all of the rest', who by definition are not directly involved with the customer transaction, but who may have an enormous degree of dependence upon it. The external stakeholders are grouped as follows:

6. *Staff*: including trade unions, individual personalities, etc.
7. *Onlookers and community*: local inhabitants, competitors, associates.
8. *Suppliers*: including those for products, loans, capital, etc.

Each of these groups is treated as external because even though they may be very involved within the organization, their views and interests may be overruled in the final analysis. They are all advisers, not decision-takers.

A galaxy

The relationships between the parts of the organization and the other interested sectors can be described as a galaxy in which all impact on one another to greater or lesser degrees. The relative strength of the constituent parts in terms of power and influence can occasionally change dramatically. If only for this reason, the response of finance to requests and needs of interested parties must always retain a degree of flexibility.

Taking the eight users identified above, a model can be developed to show the degree of interaction between the parties. Customers and consumers for the organization are shown at the centre of the system, as it is they who are the target of attention for all other parties in some way. They are the equivalent of the sun. The organization or company is closest to the customers and consumers, and here the three primary functions are shown: sales and marketing (customer contact), operations (production), and support services (infrastructure). On the outside of the organization are the other stakeholders to the transactions. Figure 3.2 shows the galaxy of users.

Finance itself plays a substantial part in the service support role and has a relationship with all of the groupings described. Some are specific (eg with bankers) and many are indirect (eg with stock market investors). All have expectations that must be identified, understood, addressed and resolved by the finance function.

Each of the sections contains customers and consumers for

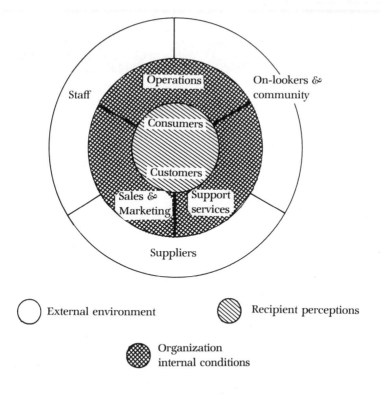

Figure 3.2 The galaxy of users

both financial information and financial services. The most usual consumers of financial functions are local management and staff who need access to financial expertise, or who make sales and purchases and wish to have the transactions recorded and completed. The customers are senior management, who decide upon the overall allocation of resources between the departments.

The model should be used to recognize the different needs of the eight different kinds of user groupings. Different techniques and skills may be required to address and solve problems within the target groups, and resources may be specifically allocated to provide solutions.

As an example, a hospital in the NHS has users that may be clearly identified in all categories:

Consumers	Patients.
Customers	The district health authority or GP fundholders who pay for the services to patients.
Sales and Marketing	The contracts department tasked to maintain and increase income generation from customers.

Operations	The surgeons, nurses and specialists that provide the care.
Support	The infrastructure of pathology, medical records, secretaries.
Staff	The personal beliefs, or ethical guidelines set out by, eg, the Royal College of Nursing, and the British Medical Council.
Onlookers	The general public, politicians, etc.
Suppliers	Corporations providing goods and services for reward.

AFFECTING CUSTOMER SATISFACTION

With an understanding of the needs and wants of the many different users, a framework for improving total satisfaction may be constructed. Practical success for finance relies on the achievement of continual and positive improvement against critical success factors (CSFs) for each grouping of user.

Within each group, success itself may have a different meaning. For this reason, Figure 3.3 opposite shows the most common measures of success that have been identified by organizations. In every case, degrees of success are measured using factors external to finance. Measurement within the three main groups is based on fundamentally different criteria, and for each user sub-group the criteria can change. The attitudes to the organization that are most likely to be adopted among users can also differ.

Critical success factors are identified so that the essence of what the user perceives as satisfying can be identified and isolated for extra or special treatment. In this way, targets and priorities can be identified and defined for each working individual and for each group of user.

The examples shown in Figure 3.3 are meant as a guide to assist readers to define the factors critical to their own success. In each case, the CSF must be an action capable of measurement by individuals working within the department.

USER ATTITUDES TO QUALITY OF SERVICE

The measurement of success by each user group will change depending upon the attitude taken by the user to the services provided. Attitudes are important because they reflect how users approach the services and information available, and will therefore give clues to finding the best methods to adopt. In recognizing the underlying implications of these user attitudes, finance will understand and address the needs and wants of all users.

	Product recipients	Internal users	External users
Users	Customers Consumers	Sales & marketing Operations Support	Staff Onlookers Community Suppliers
Critical Success Factors	Appropriate Understandable Sufficient	Accurate Concise Complete Unbiased Loyal Timely	Relevant Timely Explained Supportable Prudent Sensible Realistic
Success Measurement	Market demand	Peer pressure	Public benchmarks
Attitudes	The possible The known The safe	Political/personal goals Measured targets	Substitute

Figure 3.3   Satisfaction of users, CSFs, success and attitudes

Attitudes of product recipients

The possible: 'I am sure it is possible'

According to the normal distribution of the population, approximately 16 per cent of individuals are recognized as leaders when new ideas or concepts are available. One of the leaders' characteristics is that they are likely to buy a product simply because it is available. In a similar manner, when new financial techniques or methods become available some users demand the new item simply because it exists.

The kinds of organization that fall into this category continually test out new possibilities, systems and methods, believing that success is more likely to be achieved after trying something new. This attitude affects the finance function by creating huge volumes of unnecessary work, as resources are poured into new learning. Much effort goes into the daily routines, and frequent training is undertaken, but very little of the learning is put into practice to reduce the overall work load.

In these situations, the most productive way to manage user expectation is to declare openly a strategy of investment in new technologies and systems, one which allocates defined percentages of resources to leading edge, strategic initiatives, core work and support work. By restricting the allocation of resources to new techniques in this way, sufficient time can be released to implement the best results from new methods learned.

Users need to understand how this kind of allocation system works, and to take part in the decisions which determine which of the new techniques should be investigated. The publication of measurements which show how resources are used to operate new methods and techniques demonstrates to users the benefits of concentrating resources on implementation rather than spreading resources to learn interesting but unused techniques.

The known: 'If it is used by 500 others, it must be OK'

Approximately 68 per cent of people fall into the category where change is not necessarily welcomed. Such people need to feel secure that new concepts and techniques have been adequately tested before they try them out.

For organizations with similar characteristics, the finance function must ensure that only market leading products, commonly used techniques, and safe systems are introduced into the routines. User perceptions of the success of finance functions within this category depend upon the resilience of new systems introduced.

Over time, as the organization grows more used to changing its methods, management may gradually speed up the turnover and implementation of ideas for change and improvement.

The safe: 'Please guarantee that it will work'

The remaining 16 per cent of people in the normal population can be categorized as 'laggards'. Sometimes this group are also called 'terrorists', as they may seek to destroy initiatives if they have not been fully informed and involved in the decision-making process. They are the last to adopt new techniques and positively avoid change until absolutely necessary. Where the finance function serves this kind of individual or organization, necessity is the driver of improvement and change.

Managing organizational perceptions becomes a case of showing that the new ideas and systems have been proven, and that they are essential to the continued survival of the organization itself. As change starts to occur, the momentum for change will slowly grow.

Attitudes of internal users

Political manoeuvres

Within organizations, finance plays a key role in enabling and supporting other departments to achieve their targets and objectives. Consequently, the perceived success of the finance function internally depends upon three considerations:

1. The degree of autonomy of internal users from finance.
2. The extent of financial control required by the customers of finance (eg the directors).
3. Behavioural relationships between finance users and providers.

The degree of control required by the board of directors can sometimes create conflict for finance, especially if substantial autonomy has been delegated to operating units without sufficient trust. This is caused by two competing factors:

1. Local management belief in their own abilities.
2. Central management lack of trust in local management.

Quality attitudes will replace both of these perspectives with a common understanding and allow the parties to agree to work with beneficial compromises to the greater good. Finance is frequently the 'piggy in the middle' and has to act as an 'honest broker' in power plays. Company politics can be played by staff at all levels, and this often leads to significant inconvenience at the lower levels of seniority. High-level battles lead to lower-level damage and retaliation in which the organization itself is the loser. For this reason political perceptions should be monitored and measured among lower levels of staff, as well as within the senior ranks.

The measured response

In the few cases where internal politics can be avoided completely, specific measures of internal success can be constructed and impartially measured.

In these cases, volume of assistance, quality of assistance, skill utilization, skill development, external comparison, hindsight, speed of response, and trend analysis are all potential bases of measurement.

Measurement is discussed in greater detail in Chapter 4.

Attitudes of external users

'What if we substituted X for Y?'

External individuals and groups compare the success of an organization to potential alternatives or to what might have been possible in the light of their own objectives. Some organizations have to deal with users who imagine an alternative, eg staff thinking that they might be able to get a job elsewhere which would pay more money.

Users will therefore assess success in two ways:

1. Can a competitor (or alternative) replace the organization/ service more efficiently or effectively?
2. Has the organization fulfilled non-financial criteria effectively?

The most difficult aspect of affecting perceptions external to the organization is that the comparison could be wholly imaginary. For example, what would have been the outcome of Hanson taking over ICI in 1992? Would Zeneca have been created? In such instances the finance function must be fully aware of the environmental considerations before creating and publishing information. Figures and statistics can be shown so that users understand more of the context and application of the service or information.

THE NATURE OF CUSTOMER SATISFACTION

Whoever the customer is and whenever delivery takes place, satisfaction will never be complete. Earlier in this chapter we saw that satisfaction comprises delivery and composition. Now the human element must be added to our understanding of the users.

Over a period of time, users of an improving service will not normally recognize the improvement. This is because human memory is short, expectations can change very quickly and when improvement is achieved, the new, higher levels of expectation do not allow backward steps to be taken. Figure 3.4 expresses this natural phenomenon graphically.

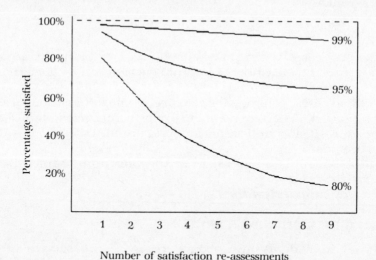

Number of satisfaction re-assessments

Figure 3.4 A snapshot of depreciating satisfaction

The curves in Figure 3.4 show how the perceptions of a single event reduce with hindsight. Something that was 'good' when it was first sampled becomes only 'acceptable' when describing it to friends later. An item that was 'OK' the first time degenerates to being only 'bearable' when telling one's colleagues a few weeks later.

Human senses recognize when things change. If the senses record consistently equal levels of sensation, that sensation is automatically reduced to background levels by the brain.

Tests prove that when individuals become used to levels of sound in the city, they will be most disconcerted when encountering an absence of sound in the countryside. This is because the background noise of the city is filtered out by the brain and has become 'normal'.

Even greater quality must be provided — perpetually

This principle of the brain normally filtering expectations applies equally to the provision of quality in services and products. As customers are provided with products and services that meet their needs more closely, they come to expect those levels to continue.

The clearest examples of this are visible in recent National Health Service developments. As a result of improvements in performance in the last 10 to 20 years, the whole UK population expects to have free access to single and multi-organ transplants. In the drive to ration health care more effectively, the availability of some of the more risky transplants has been reduced or withdrawn.

Because the public has come to expect these expensive services, an outcry has followed many of the announcements of service cuts.

Incremental improvements must be made to lift continually performance of goods and services closer to expectations. The phenomenon of continually dissatisfied customers reflects a state of 'satisfaction depreciation', which graphically is similar to the depreciation in value of assets over time.

The line created by plotting quality assessments can be one of two kinds:

1. A statement of ongoing performance.
2. A retrospective review of past performance, with the benefit of hindsight.

If one accepts that the objective of the organization is to improve customer satisfaction, there are two implications that are crucial to making real progress. These are that satisfaction:

☐ levels reduce over time (the effect of boredom);
☐ is relative to other or past services (the effect of comparison).

The better the performance, the easier is improvement

There are two ways to improve satisfaction. One is to increase the immediate user utility when the service is provided and the other is to raise the basis of assessment.

Examples of the two approaches are:

1. Increase immediate user utility by making delivery ambience more pleasing, personalizing paperwork for the user, gaining feedback personally.
2. Increase base quality by reducing standard time scales, designing improvements to standard data collection systems, improving user access to data.

These attitudes equate to 1) a car showroom being refurbished and salespeople receiving and implementing customer care training, and 2) the car models being improved to include air conditioning, ABS brakes and power steering for no extra cost to the user.

As time progresses and user expectations reflect the changes made in the quality of delivery, the difference between the best and the worst supplier is increased.

Some important implications may be drawn from this argument:

☐ The lower the initial satisfaction, the more difficult is the achievement of a prolonged, high degree of satisfaction.
☐ The higher the degree of initial satisfaction, the longer the perception will remain at high levels (ie above 80 per cent).
☐ The lower the initial satisfaction, the higher the targets of continuous improvement must be.
☐ An effort achieving an incremental improvement of, say, 5 per cent for a 100 per cent quality company would only achieve a 4 per cent incremental improvement for a comparable 80 per cent quality company.

In order to continuously improve the degree of customer satisfaction, the organization must increase the basis of assessment, while raising the routine quality of performance. The better the organization is at achieving customer satisfaction, the easier it will find the maintenance of that level of satisfaction. The rate of satisfaction depreciation is dependent upon the standards that the organization sets for itself, is prepared to fund and leads users to expect. All of the important factors in providing customer satisfaction can be altered by the providers of the service. As organizations seek to improve, the internal departmental task is to raise the measured standards, without a corresponding increase in costs.

The routes to increasing user satisfaction are therefore:

☐ providing services that meet actual needs more closely;
☐ improving internal standards of response;
☐ ensuring user recognition of improvement.

On the opposite scale, diminishing satisfaction will result from:

☐ increasing expectation, without increasing performance;

☐ failing to make constant improvement to the basic level of quality.

All of these factors demonstrate clearly that any organization cannot remain static in its drive to increase quality and user satisfaction. Measuring how quickly advance is made can be crucial to creating the feeling of success. To do this, attempts to evaluate financially any improvement are usually necessary. At this stage, a good knowledge of the environment within which services and information are provided is essential, so that the difference between the expected base quality level and the degree of user satisfaction can be shown.

DEFINING THE WORK CYCLE

The work and tasks within finance functions are complex and diverse, ranging from dealing with customers who seek to pay for goods, and agreeing with sales and marketing personnel the assumptions on which the budget for the next year might be based. Whatever work is actually completed within the finance function, a generic approach may be taken to describe that work. Working within a generic framework, there are three parts to the completion of any work:

1. The planning, deciding, reviewing and improvement cycle.
2. The task performance itself.
3. Assessing the work afterwards, to feed into item 1) again.

The most important of these parts is the planning and improvement cycle because it is here that the task to be completed is itself defined and developed. The whole infrastructure which supports delivery, systems and procedures must be constructed and developed. Through it the resulting benefits of change will be measured, monitored and assessed. The constituents of the work cycle are shown in Figure 3.5.

Feedback is the starting point for the whole cycle. From listening to problems, new solutions will be invented and evolved. By understanding and acting on feedback from users, improvements to old answers will be found and breakthrough concepts developed. Ideas are a fountain of wealth generated by customers, users and staff. Feedback is the only way of collecting the wealth of ideas to make improvement.

Evolution of the work comes from listing ideas, researching alternatives and priorities, selecting appropriate solutions and discarding the remainder. Adequate data must be gathered to ensure that the stop/go decision is the right one at the time for the organization. The more ideas that are processed at this stage the better — 99 per cent of the improvement ideas will have only a minor effect upon routine operations. Cumulatively, they will make the difference between a poor service and a brilliant

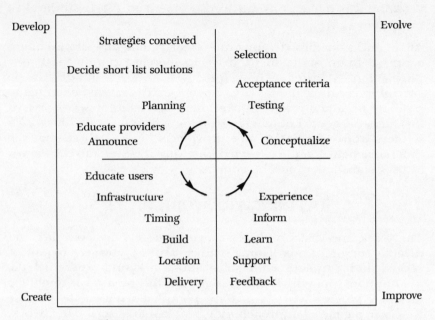

Figure 3.5 Constituents of the work cycle

service. The remaining one per cent of ideas could have a significant effect upon the organization by reducing costs, opening new markets or removing structural barriers.

Development work entails the refining and defining of improvements up to the stage of finally deciding which of the alternatives will be implemented.

Creation of the improvement occurs after the implementation decision. Actual delivery of new services or information may involve re-educating users and improving support levels.

Improvement of a service generates further feedback, and is sometimes an integral part of the creation of the provision itself, especially if the service is frequently repeated.

The result of applying the quality principles to the work cycle will be the development of the right concept, the right planning, the right support, the right delivery, and the right improvement.

4

Quality Sources

SOURCES OF QUALITY

The sources of quality are few in number, but very wide and diverse in application. The most important sources are:

☐ law;
☐ British and International Standards;
☐ institutes and self-regulation;
☐ academic teachings and political pressures.

English and European law

In the UK the most important source of fundamental quality is derived from English law. The law defines the minimum acceptable operating standards for both companies and individuals. There are major tranches of law that specifically affect the operation of finance, and in particular the operation of financial services.

The most relevant sections of the law are those relating to contracts, financial services, insolvency, companies, employment, agencies, sale of goods, and property. Recently, European Community law has increased in importance as directives take precedence over English law and the European Commission concentrates on the interface between the consumer and the supplier. In recent years UK citizens have increasingly sought legal redress in European courts.

The 1992 Maastricht Treaty created one common market from three, the European Economic Community (EEC), European Coal and Steel Community (ECSC) and the European Atomic Energy Community (Euratom). The treaty is fundamental to the legal basis of cross-border freedom of movement of goods, services and employment.

Law is an enormous subject, and this book does not deal with the legalities of finance functions or financial services, except to make the reader aware that a large part of acceptable quality standards have a basis in law.

Personal legal responsibilities have been broadened dramatically in recent legislation, especially in the 1989 Companies Act.

Severe penalties have been stipulated for persons, especially directors, who act in a wrongful or fraudulent manner. Whether they have actual financial knowledge of the status of the company is now deemed to be almost unimportant, and they can be held personally responsible for the debts of the company. The old 'veil of incorporation' has been withdrawn to a large extent.

Appendix A lists the most important statutes that apply to the finance function in some way. The list is not meant to be all-embracing, but it does cover the main Acts.

Charters

Since 1991 the UK government has increasingly publicized the standards that public utilities are supposed to meet. While the charters are not legally binding documents that are specifically enforceable in court, they have created a new management commitment to customer satisfaction. As an example, the Health Service Charter declares that the objective for the NHS is to improve the nation's health, as opposed to serving the sick.

A number of businesses have also picked up on the idea of charters for customers. It is only a matter of time before charters become legally enforceable clauses in the contract of sale.

Institutes

Over the years, the increasing volume and complexity of the law has encouraged special interest groups to form associations and institutes to help address and resolve common legal problems. As a consequence of the formation of these groups, standards have developed and minimum levels of service have been specified, below which no member should operate. These groups provide a degree of self-regulation of members, and serve three primary purposes:

1. Standardization of goods, services or behaviour.
2. Creation of new customer perception that the services from the group, are 'better' than those from other sources. This frequently leads to the group commanding a price premium.
3. Lobbying Parliament to change intended and actual legislation within the industry concerned.

Some important examples of groups which have formed associations and institutes are: barristers, solicitors, chartered accountants, chartered engineers and architects.

Institute standards generally concentrate on the general practices of members and the furtherment of trade, and usually comment on the financial implications of engaging in trade. They assume that members will abide by the law of the land first, and then add extra requirements. Entrance to a professional or regulatory institute is usually by examination, though a few have ongoing mandatory educational tests for fee-paying, qualified members. Members of institutes may be recognized in law as holding a special qualification that entitles the member to practise in a professional capacity.

Membership of the institute also generates an extra duty of care from the professional to the customer/consumer. Courts will imply an agency in law when there may not be an agency in name. Consequently, accountants may bind their client with an agreement with the Inland Revenue according to agency principles when no practical Agency exists.

Normal legal rules applying to the provision of a service are:

☐ perform with reasonable skill;
☐ within a reasonable time, if no time is specified;
☐ for a reasonable fee, if no consideration was agreed first.

These rules are extended for members of professional institutes, who are required to display 'diligence and skill'. Non-professionals need only demonstrate the abilities expected of a 'reasonable man'.

Diligence and skill can be shown through applying knowledge to the work concerned. For finance function personnel this relates to Statements of Standard Accounting Practices (SSAPs), exposure drafts and the routine specification of work prescribed by the institutes concerned. Other regulatory bodies such as FIMBRA, LAUTRO, the Stock Exchange and the Bank of England also prescribe standards that must be followed by professionals. In a limited number of cases their rules are backed up by full legal requirement, for instance in insurance underwriting, and for the clearing banks.

British Standards

To minimize the volume of legislation required to regulate industry and maximize the effect of standards, the government has developed and started to implement important minimum standards in certain products by incorporating the British Standards Institute (BSI). The BSI has prepared standard specifications for many products, which the government, as the country's largest purchaser, could practically insist upon.

By setting new minimum standards the government has sought to improve the quality of its supplies and its suppliers, the objective being an eventual reduction of its total purchasing cost. By developing the techniques of quality to apply to management, the intention was to evaluate the organization for quality in a similar way to the evaluation of a product. To achieve this the UK government copied the quality system developed by the US military. This specified how management systems could be tested and audited.

The test-bed for implementing quality strategies for both the British and US governments was their defence expenditure programmes. The earliest quality management system was recorded in the US military's 'Military Specification, Quality Program Requirements' published in 1963. The British Standards Institute brought out BS 5750 in 1979; this is a direct descendant of the American system.

The British Standards Institute have produced numerous standards relating to quality. These are:

BS 4778 Defines the quality vocabulary.

BS 5729 A guide to stock control and techniques. If your organization has a policy of holding stocks, this standard could help.

BS 5750 Parts 1 and 2 — Quality systems. Same as ISO 9000 and ISO 9001.

 The standard sets out the basics for most organizations including the 'reasons why', and the 'how to' of quality systems based on procedures.

 Organizations seeking certification must:

 ☐ decide what quality standards they will have;
 ☐ decide how to meet the standards set;
 ☐ meet the standards, monitor and report performance.

 To maintain the certificate, the organization must be able to demonstrate practical attainment of the standards through providing documentary evidence. External audit of the paperwork systems is essential to keeping the certificate.

BS 5750 Part 8 — Quality systems. Same as ISO 9004.

 An add-on to the basic British Standard, specifically produced for service organizations. Provides useful definitions and general guidance.

BS 6143 Guide to the economics of quality.

 Provides a useful framework for understanding costs of conformance, and costs of non-conformance. Emphasizes the management of processes, and explains that the critical key to managing cost is the choice of the activity parameters for defining cost drivers.

BS 7850 Total quality management

The International Standards Organization (ISO) is a body that issues standards that may be adopted internationally as a basis for the specification of goods and services. BS 5750 is the basis of the International Standards for quality management known as ISO 9000 and ISO 9001.

Total quality management

Unfortunately, total quality management (TQM) has become something of a worn cliché due to over-use and misuse since the mid-1980s. Too many companies have attempted to achieve total quality with an insufficient understanding of the meaning of total quality, and too few have been successful in achieving their own objectives.

TQM is the concept of always doing tasks right first time, every time.

The approach embraces all of the tasks within the organization ranging from cleaning the steps to selling the products, and from arranging meetings to publishing the accounts. To achieve any success, TQM is heavily reliant upon the commitment of top management and requires a change of attitude from the people that perform tasks such that their objectives change from being personally driven to being customer oriented. Successful TQM builds in customer satisfaction during production rather than adding or inspecting quality into a product or service after production is completed. It is a continuous cycle of process improvement, not one-off changes and modifications.

TQM works to eliminate the need for measuring quality, and creates an expectation of constant improvement. Techniques used in TQM include:

☐ Quality function deployment — aimed at devolving actual responsibility down to the lowest level, in order to reduce time-spans for all tasks.
☐ Benchmarking to externalize comparison — leads to generation of world class measures.
☐ Quality tools, as discussed in Chapter 9.

Within finance, the application of TQM principles results in better planning of information production and greater operator awareness of customer and user needs so that the overall cost of providing those services declines. As quality improves so finance comes to be recognized as an integral part of the services offered, and can add value for the customer. TQM is also sometimes called TQC — Total Quality Control.

As Dr K Ishikawa of Japan has said: 'TQC is a thought revolution in management, therefore the thought processes of all employees must be changed. To accomplish this, education must be repeated over and over again'.

Important prizes

Prizes are an extremely important communication tool within an organization as they demonstrate the degree of achievement of the individual or the organization, in whole or in part, as compared to other entrants in the competition. When a prize has been won, it can boost positive communication throughout the organization. The three most important international quality prizes are:

☐ Japan: The *Deming Prize* has been awarded to the company judged to be achieving the highest standards of quality in its products and services.

☐ US: The *Baldridge Award* was set up by the US Senate in 1987, partly as a response to the Deming Prize, and encourages companies to make major improvements by use of quality guidelines. The first Baldridge Prize was won jointly by Motorola, Westinghouse, and Globe Metallurgical in 1988. The criteria tested were extremely extensive and included: leadership, information and analysis, strategic quality planning, human resource utilization, quality assurance of products and services, results from QA of products and services, and customer satisfaction.

☐ Europe: The *European Quality Award* was first awarded in 1991 to Rank Xerox by the European Foundation for Quality Management (EFQM). The award was in recognition of their achievement of total quality as measured against nine main criteria: leadership (10%), processes (14%), business results (12%), People management (9%), policy strategy (8%), resources (9%), people satisfaction (9%), customer satisfaction (20%), impact on society (9%).

WHAT THE GURUS HAVE SAID

The leading international academics that have led the organizational leaders of the world toward an understanding of quality include Deming, Taguchi, Goldratt, Teboul and Juran, together with many others. These named individuals have made exceptional contributions to the concepts of quality by their books and academic works.

Many of the points that they have made can be directly applied to service functions that operate either internally or externally. A brief resumé of the salient points is given below. Where the comments cannot be translated directly into finance function performance, a brief explanation is included.

Deming — near enough is good enough

Dr Deming has written various books, the most important being *Out of the Crisis* in 1982. Deming is credited with assisting the Japanese in the 1950s and 1960s to concentrate on aspects of production by means of statistical process control (SPC), and to control quality in practical ways. He believes that employees who perform tasks are usually the best persons to resolve complex problems involving their equipment, procedures and knowledge.

Deming's 14 points provide a framework for improvement in manufacturing; the points help to a slightly lesser extent in service functions:

1. Maintain constancy of purpose of improvement — innovate, research, educate, design.
2. Adopt the new philosophy.
3. Stop depending on inspection to achieve quality.
4. Minimize total costs — use single suppliers, do not buy on price.
5. Improve constantly and forever the system of production and service.
6. Train on the job.
7. Institute leadership — help managers and workers do a better job.
8. Drive out fear of blame, retribution, etc.
9. Remove departmental barriers.
10. Eliminate slogans — eg zero defects — and work to new levels of productivity.
11. Remove management by objectives and work standards. Substitute them with genuine leadership.
12. Allow pride in the job, remove merit and production incentives.
13. Educate vigorously, allow self-improvement.
14. Everybody must achieve the transformation.

Deming invented the phrase 'statistical process control', interpreted the use of the 'normal distribution curve', and created a set of common-sense rules. He identified that the main concern was not to waste time worrying about the bottom few percentage points of production performance, but to address the problems vigorously if the process is out of control. Figure 4.1 illustrates statistical process control.

Deming pointed to many truisms that are worth quoting:

'Don't work harder, work smarter.'
'Measures of productivity do not lead to improvement in productivity.'
'Short-term profits are no index of ability.'
'Don't do your best — improve the system.'
'Slogans arise from the wrong people (management), on the supposition that with greater effort zero defects will be achieved and quality will improve.'
'If they can do it next year without a plan, why can't they do it this year?'
'Incredibly, courses and books . . . still devote time and pages to acceptance sampling.'

Dr Deming coined the mnemonic PDAC, meaning plan, do, action, check. He used this memory aid in order to help concentrate the minds of employees on the routines that should be invoked when addressing unique situations.

Example: Test results of four samples from two different processes:

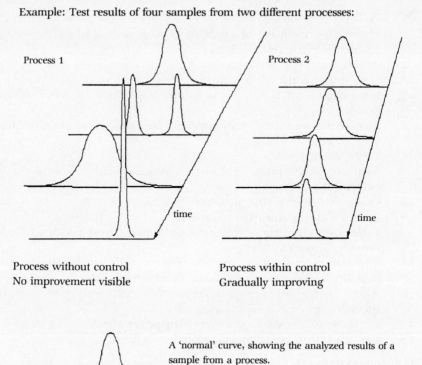

Process 1

Process 2

time

time

Process without control
No improvement visible

Process within control
Gradually improving

A 'normal' curve, showing the analyzed results of a sample from a process.

Figure 4.1 Statistical process control

Many organizations have strategies that attempt to minimize their business risk from exposure to failures of supply by spreading purchases over more than one supplier. As a result the suppliers are less able to continually lower prices because they always consider that the customer might buy elsewhere. This lack of trust between trading businesses results in responsibility being spread between several people, and sub-standard performance in work situations being accepted. This creates an expectation of failure which Deming refers to as 'the western flow'. He advises against it. Encouraging the use of single suppliers for products allows economies of scale, cross-organizational boundary economies, and the development of good business improvement relationships.

He comments: 'Don't buy on price, work with your customer and supplier.'

With regard to training he suggests that the employer should train staff in any subject in which the employee would like to be trained.

Deming advises against measuring performance and suggests that pay incentives are counter-productive. Performance should not be compared to create a league table; instead, it should simply be measured to understand where and how improvement can be made.

As authority is delegated, the necessary power to wield authority effectively should also be delegated.

The Deming principles remain true for finance function roles, probably even more so than for manufacturing. He believes that people are blamed for problems, when the cause is poor systems or processes.

For service industries, he also recognized the importance of the named individual providing the service by concurring with the statement from W E Conway, the president of Nashua Corporation: 'If you can't come send no one.'

Taguchi — go for perfection

The Japanese professor Taguchi took the ideas of delivering quality products and services further than Deming and his peers by suggesting that one must consider the whole life cycle of a product when evaluating quality. For Taguchi, quality is defined as the loss imparted to society once a product is delivered; this has become known as the 'loss function'. In his view, the loss to society because of poor design or faulty supply may be far more important than a satisfactory original delivery. To take two examples: in vehicle servicing, the more frequent the service, the greater the overall loss due to unavailability and excessive cost; a badly designed shirt will cause loss because it creates unnecessary and difficult ironing for the user.

The loss function is relevant within the finance function for both information and services. It is relevant for information because the Taguchi concepts should underlie the environmental considerations for measurement. Any discrepancy between delivery and the specified target is a problem that should be corrected.

Graphically, the loss function is shown as any difference between target performance and actual performance. This is illustrated in Figure 4.2.

The principle of loss function analysis is that the amount of deviation from target is all that matters — even the original specification of the product or service is irrelevant. Taguchi suggests that the zero defects approach is not good enough, as a defect is only defined by the criteria set by the producing personnel. The organization will gain far more from adopting a policy of 100 per cent perfection, as the underlying assumption is that identification and specification of the customers' needs must be completed in order to meet and measure perfection.

Taguchi pays a lot of attention to the design of goods and

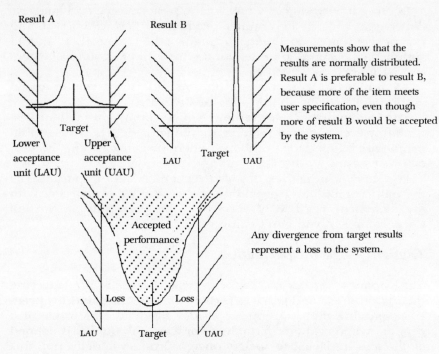

Figure 4.2 The loss funciton — Taguchi

services, and combines engineering, educated guesswork and statistical methods to achieve very rapid improvement in production and process design. By applying better design techniques, both cost reduction and quality improvement of products become possible.

Taguchi states that it is important to know where a measurement starts, because any changes may then be measured. The measured change represents the practical effect of the last modification to the system, parameters or tolerances. He developed clear rules for testing designs, parameters and tolerances so that the cause of shift in measurements can be isolated. For manufacturing, his view was that management must improve:

☐ System design: don't use statistics alone, use the appropriate technology for the job, prototype the system, changes and improvements.

☐ Parameter design: use experimental design methods to find the optimum settings for the parameters within the system.

☐ Tolerance design: use experimental design methods to set tolerance band widths within the system.

The definition of experimental design is the use of lateral thinking, informed guess-work, and try it and see methods. From the modification of the four main factors involved in a process, discover the factor that has the maximum effect on the target and the parameters that have been set. Once discovered, zoom in on this factor and make improvements.

Taguchi advises us, when identifying the controllable factors, to ignore the 'noise' that always surrounds experiment and modification. Optimum levels for the controllable variables may be set to ensure that the system, and its parameters and tolerances, are all defined with maximum regard to the impact of the variables upon their mutual performance.

Goldratt and achieving business objectives

Goldratt's *The Goal* and *The Race* are both books which clearly explain the operational importance of planning, error-free production, set-up times and clean-up times in manufacturing environments. These principles apply directly to any service function — indeed to any operation at all. Though Goldratt is not specifically identified with the quality movement, the relevance of his writings lie at the core of any quality initiative. Some quotations from his books are worth repeating:

'The goal is to reduce operational expense, and to reduce inventory while simultaneously increasing throughput.'
'Most factors critical to running a plant can be determined in advance.'

About quality:

'If I told you what to do, ultimately you would fail.'

Looking at the build up of work in progress at machines:

'What's happening isn't an averaging out of fluctuations in various speeds, but an accumulation of the fluctuations. Mostly it is an accumulation of slowness, because dependency [between machines] limits opportunity for higher fluctuations.'

The principle of demand-controlled manufacturing is that averages in planning cannot work, so Goldratt uses planning to avoid using the law of averages. You can test the failure of the law of averages for yourself:

Imagine that five people sit round in a circle. One person rolls the dice and moves the number of matches shown on the dice to the person on their left, together with the dice. The fifth person should eject matches into a 'finished' counting bowl.
Continue this process for five rounds. At this point the law of averages suggests that 17 or 18 matches will have been put into circulation.
Although the numbers input to the system may well equal the expected (average of 3.5 per round, equals 18), you will find that most of the component matches are still in the system.
The law of averages has clearly broken down as more matches should have been ejected from the closed system.
Mathematically, there is only a 3 per cent probability of three

or more matches completing the cycle after round one. Try it for yourself to see what happens as the test progresses.

Applying this matchstick phenomenon to services shows that the greater the pile of work that is waiting to be done on any one desk, the more processes there are waiting for items to be completed at that bottleneck process. To solve these timing and bottleneck problems, Goldratt suggests three rules:

1. Match the overall speed to that of the slowest process.
2. Do not balance capacity with demand, balance the flow with demand (eg a plant with the capacity to produce 50m bottles per annum is useless if 10m bottles will be required in one week).
3. Solve the problems at the bottleneck machines, do not waste time considering secondary problems at non-bottleneck machines.

As a general rule, by finding the biggest stack of unfinished or unstarted work at any one machine, you have found the bottleneck machine for the plant.

Translating these principles to services — people are the equivalent of machines. The greater the skill of an individual, the more likely they are to be a bottleneck because fewer people are able to provide alternative working capacity. Goldratt states that most calculations of machine hourly costs are incorrect 'not because of calculation error, but because the costs were determined as if the work centre existed in isolation. An hour lost at a bottleneck is an hour lost to the entire system.'

This has significant implications for the pricing and cross-charging of time for most support services such as finance. Of course, there is also the fact that as more bottleneck problems are solved, you then automatically create new bottlenecks elsewhere. The point that most people forget when addressing this problem is that by solving bottleneck problems they are actually increasing total capacity capability.

Goldratt and costing

In services, if the only individual that can provide the services demanded by the user has a holiday, the whole system stops. Costing the time of that person at merely their hourly rate of pay would fail to recognize the effect of their efforts on the whole organization.

In manufacturing, management have historically allowed under-utilized machines to work at their optimum capacity to obtain budgeted or peak 'efficiency' levels. This approach is a response to the human desire to see people working, rather than to see the production of benefit. Such errors create unnecessary stock and work in progress (WIP) at the bottleneck units, and extra costs are routinely incurred to resolve problems.

The simplest route to avoiding WIP is to introduce 'pull'

systems that only request components for delivery when they will be required. The pull system generates smaller supplier order batches and lower numbers of completed units ready for shipment. These principles can be applied to services by requiring the personnel that provide a service to be forward thinking and to plan their service provision better.

Goldratt also states: 'Don't assume that because somebody is working that you are gaining any benefit.'

He explains in simplistic terms the principles of just in time (JIT) manufacturing, in which stock is treated as an absolute evil, all production is the result of pulled demand and unnecessary production is avoided.

He defines the concept of bottleneck machines, and illustrates how the bottleneck machine can change as frequently as production schedules changes. The slowest machine drives the total maximum capacity of the plant, assuming that all production has to go through all of the machines.

Goldratt highlights the importance of flexibility of order taking. If orders taken range between, say, 100 and 5,000 per day, this can generate problems because the system must be flexible enough to maintain delivery. Education of the customer may be more appropriate in these circumstances than huge new capital expenditure to meet widely fluctuating demand patterns.

To increase and improve production, set-up times and clean-up times are crucial. The more that these non-productive times are reduced, the more capacity is freely created for the organization. Reductions of 60–90 per cent in both set-up and clean-up times are not uncommon initial rates of improvement.

The repair and maintenance of plant is important, but when breakdowns occur the cause of the problem is far important than the physical repair. Total production maintenance (TPM) is the name given to the system by which breakdowns and the resolution of maintenance problems can be managed according to quality principles.

Economic order quantities (EOQ) represents false mathematics and leads to waste because it fails to recognize that demand drives orders, not production. The economics of this is that where set-up times and clean-up times are reduced to zero, there is no benefit in producing more than one unit at a time.

When reviewing processes, management should focus on and reduce any non-value added work. Effectiveness is crucially more important than efficiency.

Others

Juran

Like most of the writers on quality, Juran's principles can add value to the finance function if one translates the production-oriented comments to finance function requirements.

Juran pointed out that quality ratings have historically been based on the evaluation of product features rather than the benefits for the customer. This has led to numerous errors, especially in the retail trade, because surveys have found that customer satisfaction is more related to sensory perceptions (eg colour or pattern) than to functionality. For services, this knowledge supports the view that the manner of delivery may be more important than the content of the delivery.

Juran also noted that when companies add degrees of perfection beyond the perceived level of functionality required, no value is added, only cost. Important examples are building products that have been engineered to last beyond their expected obsolescence dates; expensive finishes on non-visible surfaces; and unduly large factors of safety.

Juran suggests analyzing value added by activity, recommending the use of flow-chart analysis to help identify all of the processes. To help decide whether processes are necessary, important or superfluous he suggested the completion of the form shown in Figure 4.3 for each activity.

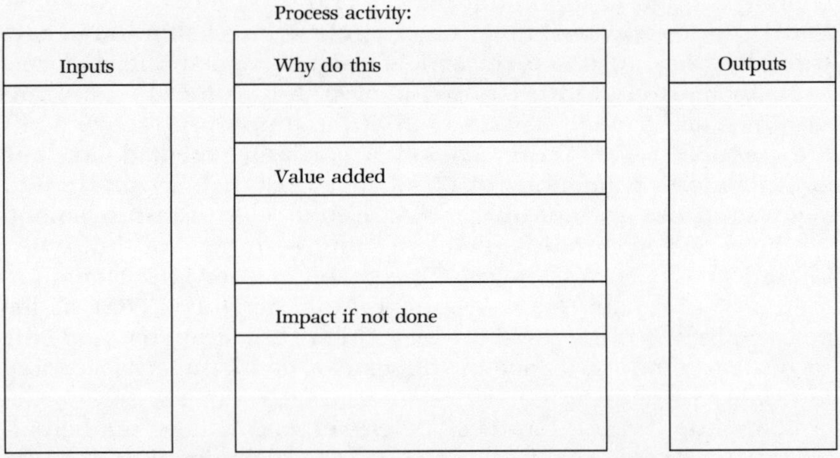

Process activity:

Inputs	Why do this	Outputs
	Value added	
	Impact if not done	

Figure 4.3 Analyzing value added by activity

Teboul

Teboul introduced the concept of 'The 5 Olympic Zeros'. These are points where the organization sets internal objectives of reducing to zero the measured units of:

☐ defects;
☐ delay;
☐ inventory;
☐ breakdown;
☐ paper.

In order to make the achievements practicable there must be an incontestable reason for change. Without such a reason, there will be insufficient agreement between staff concerning the extent of action to take. Identifying these reasons may be straightforward in most cases, but in others 'pump priming' may be necessary. A need for change must be generated, or a crisis created.

The other criteria that must be present include:

☐ management commitment;
☐ trust;
☐ promotion and training.

The system of implementation should:

☐ pilot, experiment and create champions.

Teboul emphasized the importance of providing employees with enough room to grow intellectually and in terms of responsibility, in order to minimize internal resistance to change. Managers must first gain the overall quality vision for themselves, and then disseminate that vision among all of the staff. Various tools are needed to assist the communication process, and graphic modelling may be appropriate in many organizations to help the early achievement of a common understanding among staff.

Teboul constructed the technique called FMEA — failure mode and effect analysis. In this technique, complex products are taken apart in order to classify all potential problems. Findings are scored and prioritized against three criteria:

☐ severity of failure;
☐ probability of recurrence;
☐ probability of non-detection.

This technique is especially useful for evaluating risk associated with complex products (eg cars) and does not easily translate to finance function services. However, in constructing adequate environments for information, similar techniques are used to assess the potential for particular outcomes in forecasting (eg wars, riot, floods).

Teboul highlighted the benefits of generating a culture that does not accept failure, and demonstrated the effects mathematically. The more complex a product or service, the more important it is for the organization to accept zero failures of performance. For those organizations that accept 1 per cent of their output as failures, the calculations are as follows:

The likelihood of producing 100% perfect product $= (P)^n$

Where P = probability of individual item success
and n = number of components in the final product.

For a 99% company with 50 components in the product, the expectation of success is:

$(0.99)^{50} = 0.60 =$ success expectation of 60%.

Therefore the *expectation of failure is 40%*.
For a 99% company with 1,000 components in the product:

$(0.99)^{1,000} = 0.00004 =$ success expectation of 0.004%

Therefore the *expectation of failure is 100%*

Financial services are extremely complex products which may demand the provision of many subordinate components operating together to provide the service perfectly. When the service is continually repeated (like insurance or credit control), the reliability of secondary elements must be very high.

For financial information, large volumes of data are inherent to the service provided, which is therefore at a greater risk of error or failure.

The application of mathematical principles shows that failures at any level are not acceptable.

5

Rule Book

QUALITY IS THE ATMOSPHERE, NOT THE VISION

Many people mistakenly believe that quality is the ultimate objective of their organization. The fact is that organizations only exist to fulfil the needs of their stakeholders, customers and consumers as expressed by their mission statements. Quality is the atmosphere within which better achievement will be possible, and through which improvement is managed.

The atmosphere of quality is expressed through the words and actions of the company. The words are those defined by the board, management or staff and are found in the mission statements, objectives and targets. Each of the statements informs the one below it, eventually producing instructions which limit or facilitate action. To fully understand the differences between the statements, we define them here:

Mission   an expression of the reason for the existence of the organization.

Values   the statement of the philosophy of the organization which underlies the existence of the corporate body. These are equivalent to the assumptions that underpin financial statements.

Objectives   the conditions to which the organization aspires, expressed in quantifiable terms, usually requiring achievement within a defined period of time.

Targets   are specific, measurable criteria, against which progress may be plotted. Frequently expressed for individuals, parts of the organization, and for the whole.

Methods   the actions and routes that propel the organization toward its targets.

Quality principles should be applied to each of the statements as they are created and enacted. The creation of statements is important to the generation of a commonly-held series of goals within the organization. If the staff have nothing written down to which they may refer later, ideas and recommendations for progress simply become so much more hot air.

The content of these documents is outlined below:

The mission is normally created by the board of directors after consultation with the different stakeholders if the organization is already established, or from personal belief when the organization is a new one. Not all organizations need a mission, especially when they are set up to achieve one sole objective before being wound up, eg some charities.

Some organizations confuse their objectives, for their mission.

Values arise when a number of individuals work together to achieve some particular objective. As the organization grows it will assume a set of beliefs and values, resulting from a consensus of opinion.

Over a period of time values may change, though many firms actively discourage changes to their value system. For many organizations their values and beliefs translate directly into the statement of company ethics, eg the adoption in 1992 by the Co-op bank of 'green' values when lending or investing funds.

Some chief executive officers (CEOs) see the destruction of old value systems as essential to the survival of the company, and actively seek to destroy and then replace them with more appropriate beliefs.

Objectives are defined by the board when individuals or the organization need to achieve something specific. For many companies the objectives relate directly to the contents of the Memorandum and Articles of Association.

Many departments prepare their own sets of objectives, and apply them to help achieve the ultimate aims of the organization.

Targets are frequently specified as a result of discussion between those who created the vision (the directors) and those who will report the practical achievements (the managers). These represent milestones that mark the advancement of the organization in specific and measured ways.

Methods are the practical structures by which operational management work toward the objectives, to best achieve the targets.

Organizational structure, committees, decision-making processes, policies, standards and procedures are all methodologies.

Statements defining the mission and the organizational values are normally the responsibility of the board of directors or equivalent. The most advanced finance functions have progressed to the stage where they have prepared their own mission and value statements.

The statements cascade responsibility, authority and limitations down through the management ranks. At all levels the statements become the means by which the organization progresses in a logical and ordered manner.

Quality is the word used to understand the method by which all these functions and operations may be planned, undertaken, assessed and improved. A deeper understanding of the relationship between the cascade of statements, the quality initiatives and the organization can be achieved by analogy with travelling:

Statement	Travel analogy
Mission	The reason for travelling
Values	The attitude of the travellers
Objectives	The destination
Targets	Milestones on the way
Methods	Means of transport

Customer perceptions are represented by the weather that the traveller may encounter, and expectations are the difficult and changing terrain that must be traversed.

Many companies use the term 'quality tools' to describe special methods and techniques that they use to assist achievement. These are in many ways the equivalent of the map, compass, watch, binoculars and other equipment that may be required for the journey. The use of quality tools helps staff to communicate in the same language, and to understand the direction, destination and progress much more readily.

THE BASIC QUALITY PRINCIPLES

Before any organization can provide added value for customers, an infrastructure must be in place to provide and support the good or service. The finance function is central to the infrastructure of any organization and, due to its complex nature and the interrelated aspects of the functions, requires both capacity and demand planning. Operational flexibility is required to allow staff to provide individual attention and service to every user, in every product and service, every time.

Developing from the definition of quality within the finance function, the application of quality principles to the foundations of the infrastructure creates a series of ground rules. The degree of satisfaction that will be perceived by the user will depend on the success of operating within these rules.

The eight rules and a brief analysis of them are listed below; they are discussed in more detail later in this chapter.

1 Understand your business

Within financial services a clear knowledge of precisely what is being provided to customers is essential. Usually this entails asking the users and customers their opinion in surveys, as employees and other staff have biased opinions.

For financial information this means understanding how the core data arises, how it can be gathered, and how information is built up.

When data is reliably sourced, automation can usually be applied very swiftly.

2 Process once, promptly and correctly: data quality

Gathered data must be processed efficiently, once only. Whether the accounting systems are manually or computer run, they penalize error by causing time wasting when an imbalance or problem occurs.

As computers are unable to spot simple coding errors, problems can be magnified to immense proportions, especially when this involves statistical inaccuracy — staff usually pay much more attention to value than volume.

The cost of error correction is huge, because specialist expertise is usually required in addition to extra consultation with the originator of the error.

A number of organizations have developed their thinking to the extent that staff are encouraged to take more time to process documents, to get them right all of the time. They realize that effectiveness at first leads to efficiency later.

3 Find out what the user/customer wants: presentation quality

From good communication with users a solid understanding can be gained of how needs can be fulfilled.

Working without quality leads to many reports being produced for users without an understanding of what is required. Many unnecessary and incorrectly formatted reports are produced, resulting in a waste of time, effort and resource.

Users rarely need routine detailed information when events are progressing according to plan or schedule. Exception reports and summaries are usually of much greater utility to the user.

4 Check that the reporting environment is adequate and complete: environment quality

Exercising the professional duty of care to define data content properly, and the checking of knock-on and peripheral implications are part of the environmental concerns. Alternatives should have been addressed and included where relevant.

Presentation of information is a central element to comprehension by the user. Recognize that other users are likely to see the information, not just the intended user.

5   Ensure that the user interprets and acts upon the information correctly: decision quality

The task of reading and interpreting data and information can range from being a simple task to one of great complexity.

The degree of the user's financial skill must be assessed and matched to the resulting report in order to generate the best decision in given circumstances.

Many organizations may discover that the greatest degree of skill is required at the lowest level of decision-making until the junior management responsible for the process have learned how to apply the financial techniques for themselves.

6   Meet the needs accurately, timely, and constantly

The fundamental accuracy of the underlying data within reports has to be checked, and is always best done before publication.

The necessity for reporting should be checked regularly with users in a review of the timeliness and effectiveness of the service.

When defining the high level deadlines for systems to be closed for reporting purposes, allow sufficient time for intermediate level and lower level tasks to be completed. Period end cut off should not be too early.

When frequent reports are required, they should be produced through routine performance. They should not be the result of specialist, one-off tasks completed frequently.

7   Make constant improvements

By introducing process change and process review to the organization, and keeping change happening, the culture will grow to *expect* change. Expectation will lead to higher and further improvement, and a virtuous circle will have been created.

8   Empower performance

Empowerment takes place when supervision is removed from operators. The performance of each individual becomes critical to the whole organization and system of service. Failure is not acceptable.

Empowered staff have been given the responsibility and authority to decide what tasks should be performed, and then to perform them.

Ground rule 1: understand your own business

A tower block relies on its foundations being solid and immobile, designed to withstand huge pressures from above. In the same way, finance functions must have stable foundations for their core data, designed to provide services and information supporting many user requirements.

For our purposes, we will break the function into two parts, the provision of:

1.   financial services;
2.   financial information.

Understanding financial services — back room or front office?

The distance between the location of the finance services and external customers affects the selection of the most appropriate way to achieve improvement. The nearer the customer, the more important are interpersonal skills, whereas the further from the customer, the greater the demand for data skills.

A grid which helps to identify the main factors affecting the role of the finance function services is illustrated in Figure 5.1.

This grid may be used to decide priorities, to recognize which events are more crucial to customers and users, and to help identify the critical success factors for the event and function.

Understanding financial information

Core financial information can be said to have four elements:

1. price and value data;
2. descriptive data;
3. volume and statistical data;
4. coding, allocation and authorization details internal to the organization.

Though the first three elements are normally visible on the face of any sales or purchase invoice, a surprising number of computer systems fail to allow volume or statistical data to be held in the same section of the account as financial data. This omission leads to duplication, errors and problems in information reporting.

The fourth element of allocation, coding and authorization, is only used internally. The 'chart of accounts' is the name given to the complete listing of all possible allocation alternatives, and defines the form of the costing structure and income profile of the organization. This code is the method by which items in elements 1, 2 and 3 can be reported on, making up the basic information on which decisions can be based.

Poorly designed charts of accounts create and multiply potential for future errors. One national company that introduced a 19-digit cost code estimated that 30 per cent of all original entries in the first year required correction. By year 3, errors had fallen to less than 5 per cent, but this error rate was still unacceptably high.

If the basis of the data or the understanding of the data is flawed, the potential is greatly increased for defective decisions which adversely affect the whole organization.

Trend analysis is essential to successful reporting so that degrees of success can be gauged. For those bodies involved in a great deal of organizational change, code structures require exceptionally tight control so that trends are not lost as internal structures change. Cost codes must be designed carefully, both to

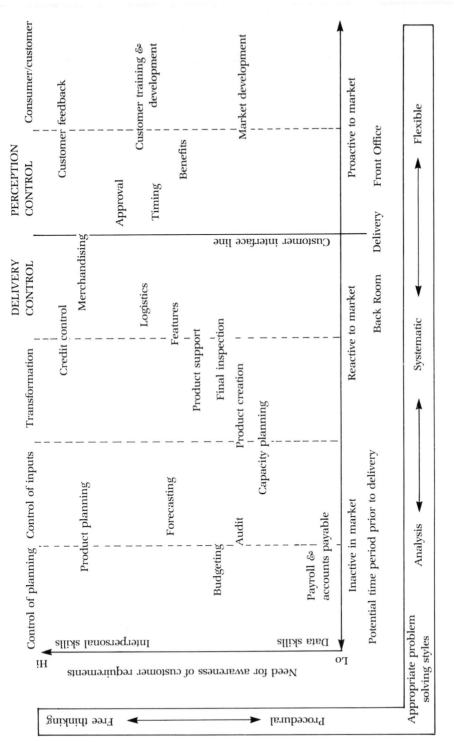

Figure 5.1 Positioning of finance — back room or front office?

allow for later modification and variation of reports to provide comparisons, and to allow the restatement of previously published information. Trend progress from one year to the next may then be reported, regardless of the new organizational structure. When an organization is going through major changes, the importance of reliable base data cannot be overemphasized.

The chart of accounts provides users with a framework for comprehending both the whole organization and its constituent parts. When designed with common sense, the hierarchy of accounts and the relationships between codes gives an insight into the priorities of the organization, and where management focus lies. Statistics and the financial dynamics form an essential part of that understanding; both are necessary to a full understanding of the business. Relationships between events may be obvious to those who perform operational functions, but to other decision-makers, the relationship may not be clear.

Finance personnel have unique access to the complete organizational structure, and can ensure that internal communication and understanding within the organization is maximized.

Ground rule 2: process once, promptly and correctly

The rules of minimal processing are the same for both service providers and the information providers — Get it right first time.

Many organizations process information many, many times. There are occasions when the same information is processed in the same department by the same people several times, simply to produce slightly different reports. Some companies even develop major computer systems, linked electronically, which duplicate complete sets of basic information. Duplication has several detrimental effects:

- □   increased cost of setting up data;
- □   increased cost of maintenance and update of base data;
- □   danger of introduction of error, or failure to discover omissions;
- □   danger of using incorrect information.

By removing duplication, many finance functions could make substantial savings in time and money very quickly. For example, in 1993, in a division of a large national utility company, the finance function ran separate systems for: the general ledgers; a system for project management; a linked system to control project costs; a different system to control staff time allocation; and a system to control payroll. Some systems were local, others centrally operated. In addition, large Lotus 1-2-3 spreadsheets were used locally to report actual expenditures, because none of the main systems provided sufficient data in the right format.

When data is collected and input to a system, the best point of control is at the earliest point of entry into the system. We discuss this in the next chapter. Personal responsibility reduces or avoids the possibility of inaccuracy, and tends to standardize the kinds of input methods to the systems. Many companies have moved away from central data processing facilities to devolved input screens for staff to input information directly. Examples are computerized tills in public houses and bar code readers in large warehouses.

Where local input of data has been introduced, the higher degree of personal responsibility has had a dramatic impact on the basic accuracy of the data. Personal objectives, targets and methods have then been introduced to help individuals continue to improve their performance.

Where responsibility has not been devolved, staff tend to believe in the accuracy of computer print-outs unless an error is blindingly obvious, and usually no one wants to take responsibility for problems when they are uncovered. This results in many reports going unchecked to the users, and errors being directly incorporated into decision-making. When errors are found, resources have to be diverted from other important tasks to make the necessary corrections, which can have substantial direct and indirect implications, and which will detract from the main purpose of the organization.

Ground rule 3: find out what the user wants

Te first problem here is to correctly identify the user of the service or information to be provided. Chapter 3 discussed these points.

Users usually want the service or information to be provided in a calm and clear manner, within a specified timetable. Discovering the details of what is required differs according to whether financial services or financial information is to be provided.

Financial services

For financial services, the ultimate consumer of the service is located outside the organization, and could be a customer of the organization as a whole. In these cases the financial service should be treated as a core part of the product or service of the organization. The fact that money is involved should not cloud the fact that it is part of the whole interface with external customers.

Debtors can be helped to pay promptly and shown how not to pay late in future; suppliers can be helped by making prompt payments in return for discounts or special concessions.

When the consumer is internal, the customer is the management of the organization itself. The specification of required services is frequently overlooked by internal finance functions and the recharge of cost lacks a direct relationship between utility and value added. Conflict is thus introduced because some consumer sections may complain that charges bear no relation to the utilization of services. The main benefit of providing internal consumers with financial services should be that needs can be more fully and readily met. A number of organizations have introduced internal trading agreement systems to resolve and clarify the use that can be made of internal services.

Financial information

Never start to produce information or take action until the requirements of the user are clear. Partial explanation and inadequate descriptions lead to wasted effort, unless a strategy of incremental development has been decided upon from the beginning.

User requirements should be understood in the overall context within which the user must work. This means identifying the ultimate objective of the user because only by understanding the final aim can an entire and satisfactory environment be constructed for the information. Where the users are unsure of their requirements, professional skill and judgement should be applied to generate an environment of information which will allow them to find their own goals. Incremental approaches that constantly refer back to the users for affirmation, even though time-consuming, will produce the best and quickest results for both parties. In many cases, users find it helpful if a statement of need has been produced to categorize:

☐   the purpose of the information;
☐   basic data required, including accuracy, completeness, etc.
☐   presentation criteria, covering things like format, regularity, and timeliness;
☐   the environmental data, including assumptions and implications.

Information should be presented in a pre-defined style that has been agreed with users to meet their own communication needs. Some organizations have developed reporting formats that help users to recognize the most suitable presentation of the information.

Many users will not be aware of the amount of work that may go into providing decision support and assistance. By making internal users aware of the work content, overall effectiveness will improve substantially, especially if payment for the service is required. For external users, a balance must be struck between the cost of providing information and the cost of not providing it.

There are two further environmental considerations that should not be overlooked:

1.   The degree of certainty that is sought or expected by the user. Risk is likely to change significantly from project to project,

so risk analysis should be incorporated into the provision process.
2.   The level of detail and complexity of the information.

Responsible management of the presentation of these variables will result in the matching of supply with expectation.

Ground rule 4: check that the environment is adequate and complete

The framework within which a service is supplied is its environment. To ensure that the service will make sense to the user, the provider must apply common sense to a review of the service (see also Chapter 2).

Financial information

Where information is to be provided, peripheral data may be required so that sense can be made of the information. For example, the forecast of the US dollar price of oil for the next six months has little value to a UK fuel retailer unless forward exchange rates are also quoted.

When providing information, supplying a copy of the underlying assumptions demonstrates to users that care has been taken in preparing the data. Being able to see assumptions and important related criteria allows users to modify or adjust any of the figures to meet their needs more closely.

Financial services

The environment for service provision includes the events that lead up to the involvement of finance, such as the terms and conditions of sale, contractual obligations and the credit rating of suppliers.

The ambience to the provision of the service should be conducive to helping users achieve the satisfaction that they seek. There would be little point in providing private and discreet financial consultancy services from a desk based on the platform at Liverpool Street Station.

After the service has been performed, information relating to the service and its result must be collected so that assessment, evaluation and learning may take place. From each provision of a service some lesson should be identified and acted upon.

Generally, financial service provision calls for high degrees of interpersonal skills from service staff so that they can provide flexible responses to meet customer demand. Employees must have advanced listening skills so that they will hear, and be able to understand and act upon their new knowledge.

The final test for goods, services and information is that of 'fitness for purpose'. Those working in the finance function should always check their service before it is delivered to make sure that it will provide the user with what is wanted.

Ground rule 5: ensure that the user interprets the information correctly

A large part of standard financial training is the development of statistical interpretation skills. These skills are only of value when they are communicated successfully to the user. An essential point to get across to users is the fact that numbers are mere representations of the facts of operations and business. Understanding what the numbers mean does not entitle the interpreter to actually take the decisions. In its capacity as interpreter, the finance function does not take operational decisions.

Users recognize that finance is only one aspect of their decision-making process, although it is frequently believed to be the most important aspect. They know that a full understanding of the underlying causes and implications of figures and statistics will improve their decision-making.

Some information required by users is extremely complex and a high degree of skill is needed to interpret the data meaningfully. This is especially true where decisions could have significant implications for other figures and statistics within the business, and relationships are not immediately visible from the information presented. Finance functions must therefore match the financial skills of the staff available to the roles and tasks requested by the user. As more responsibility is devolved down to lower management levels, greater expertise will be required at those lower levels. For some organizations this will require a reassessment of the skills of their financial staff, and consideration of where they should be applied to achieve the best results.

Ground rule 6: meet the needs effectively, accurately, timely and constantly

Meeting the needs of users effectively is more important than operating the function with great efficiency. This is because the drive for efficiency pays too much attention to the details of calculations and processes, and too little attention to meeting the original needs.

Effectiveness equals:

□ fitness for the purpose — constantly;
□ added value for the user;
□ timeliness in presentation;
□ accuracy and completeness.

Efficiency is internal to the finance function, and relates to:

- ☐ revenue benefit for the department, over cost;
- ☐ utilization of skills and resources;
- ☐ systematic, logical and repeatable methods to resolve problems;
- ☐ keeping the improvement cycle turning.

Common areas that lead to failure to meet the needs of users fall into four categories:

1. Communication: poor presentation, resulting in a lack of clarity, or not making the purpose clear.
2. Underlying assumptions: objectives may change; so may the environment.
3. Definition of requirements: measurements and requirements may be flawed.
4. Timing: overlaps, delays, problems.

Ground rule 7: make constant improvements

Change is the key word within quality because practical accomplishment of change is the crucial issue. Only by implementing recommendations will benefits be achieved, savings made and user satisfaction constantly improved. Only through change will the organization actually make those improvements. Historical attitudes of opposition to any change from within the finance function must be completely and utterly reversed.

Positive change must be sought out and implemented.

The budgeting process bind policies and procedures into a 12-month timetable. There is little reason for organizations to allow change to take so long; if improvement can be made in three months, then why allow one year?

Financial services

Improving the service delivery is relatively straightforward once a clear understanding has been reached of precisely what the service consists of. A logical system of component improvement may then be installed and implemented. In order to create such a system an understanding of the user's mission must first be achieved, so that all improvements may be prioritized against objectives. Improvements should be made to all parts of the delivery and content of the service — for the benefit of the user, not the provider.

Service improvement should relate to increases in the effectiveness of the service itself. Only when the service is effective and in continuous demand should resources be directed at improving efficiency. This is because users will normally be responsible for deciding whether the service meets their needs; whether it is cost-effective is a secondary consideration.

Internal customers demand efficiency because they ultimately pay for all of the department's costs and so any reduction in cost is usually welcomed. There are distinct advantages to considering whether the function should be subcontracted out because it will propel users into actually deciding the levels of service they require from the finance function.

Financial information

To improve effectiveness for information users, attention should be directed at the:

- [ ] appearance and manner of communication;
- [ ] basic data included;
- [ ] complexity and level of understanding required;
- [ ] alternatives considered within the report;
- [ ] conclusions and recommendations;
- [ ] environmental considerations.

Efficiency in the production of information may be addressed by applying quality tools. Three important items to consider are:

- [ ] methods and processes used;
- [ ] resources consumed;
- [ ] match of skills to requirements.

When creating information or products, do not wait until output has been perfected; the wait could take for ever. Because the costs of production always escalate in proportion to the time consumed, the benefit resulting from the added degree of perfection is extremely unlikely to offset the additional cost.

Ground rule 8: empower performance

A crucial aspect of general management is the creation of a working environment in which employees may work constructively and positively in order to generate real benefits for the employers and without requiring constant intervention from supervisors and management.

Empowerment is where supervision of staff is removed and the performance of the individual becomes essential to the well-being of the organization. Within finance this principle can cause control-oriented individuals to refuse to implement change, in the flawed belief that employees cannot be trusted. To overcome this difficult attitude the following points should be considered:

- [ ] A single error is caused by either a lack of experience and learning, or by a faulty process.
- [ ] The second error is caused by a lack of understanding and education.
- [ ] The third error is caused by incompetence.
- [ ] Controlling performance more than once is wasteful.
- [ ] How many errors should the customer pay for?

The opinions expressed above show how failure can be graded in order to decide how to put problems right. In the light of those grades management and staff can assess the seriousness of the problem and how the system can be improved.

Four principles should be adopted to empower employees:

1. Trust — allow the freedom to perform and improve.
2. Teach — encourage, train and develop.
3. Delegate — pass responsibility and authority to those who require it.
4. Discipline — enforce control on the direction and speed of action.

The extent to which these principles are adopted will depend upon the vision of management (financial and non-financial), the ability of the organization and the current state of quality achievement. Adopting these principles could introduce a degree of conflict, however. Financial services require control because of the danger of theft, collusion and misappropriation of funds. Financial information requires freedom to change and improve data and information so that the best decisions may be enacted.

Managing conflicting interests is a normal part of human activity. Adopting the principles of empowerment does not create new conflict, it merely recognizes old conflict.

From adopting these principles of empowerment, the finance function can achieve impressive benefits from improved effectiveness and efficiency.

IDENTIFYING QUALITY PROGRESS IN FINANCE

A number of far-sighted organizations have recognized that quality in finance functions has numerous component parts. These component parts can be grouped under the following headings:

1. Data quality.
2. Presentation quality.
3. Decision-making quality.

These primary levels of financial quality can exist in organizations with or without quality initiatives elsewhere in the organization. However, presentation quality cannot fully exist without data quality, and decision-making quality cannot exist without both presentation and data quality. By putting organizational quality and finance quality together, a framework to aid decisions may be generated. This is illustrated in Figure 5.2.

In Figure 5.2, the term 'engineering' is used to denote technical competence within the company, and not any specific engineering competence. The figure shows how the state of quality within an organization may be assessed in relation to the quality

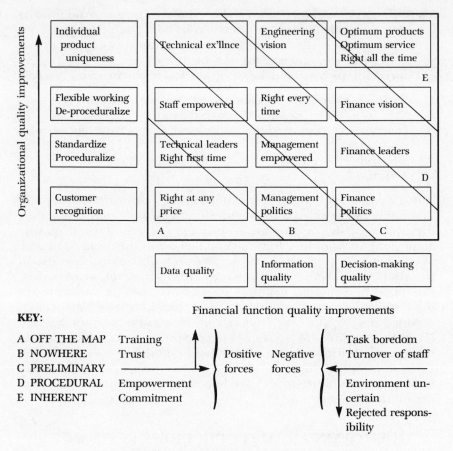

Figure 5.2 Identifying quality progress

initiatives in the finance function and in the organization as a whole. It indicates the degrees of change in attitude that reflect advancement from the lowest quality grades to the highest.

The more powerful and visionary the finance function leader, the further to the right of the chart is the position of the organization. The more thoroughly quality pervades the organization, the higher is its positioning on the chart.

By recognizing the strengths and weaknesses of the organization in this way, a strategy for improving and changing its position can be constructed.

6

Considering the People

LEADERSHIP

The most critical part of any quality project is the competence, communication skills and vision of those who lead the initiative. These are the main leadership qualities of any major quality initiative that will achieve success. There are a few brilliant individuals in UK organizations who are leading the way forward to quality in the finance function, and the rest of the world has to follow. These leaders have seen that 'best-shot' management is not good enough and that clear, accurate and fast responses will ultimately win through.

The path to excellence is rarely smooth and simple and the personal style of the individual is frequently misread and misunderstood. Messages of trust can be seen as political manoeuvring, and the offer of empowerment can be disbelieved and disdained. Failure results from a mismatch of leadership style with organizational need. Within quality environments the problem of matching leadership style to organizational need is made more complex because of the cynicism of staff that have 'seen it all before'.

Depending upon how advanced quality initiatives are within the organization, the style of leadership must change to reflect the differing needs of staff that have not advanced up the quality ladder as far as their colleagues. Adoption of the wrong approach will result in conflict between the leader and the other parties.

For example:

1. An autocratic style adopted to lead the organization 'out of the wilderness' by the adoption of quality attitudes and procedures will fail if applied to the stage of proceduralization.

    This is because autocrats will seek to centre power upon themselves and neglect to pass authority and responsibility to others. The autocrat must become a facilitator so that others begin to move towards quality attitudes and beliefs by starting to think for themselves.
2. A totalitarian communist style (intent on standardizing all 1products, output and procedures down to the very last detail) will succeed in bringing order and understanding early in the

initiative, but will fail as the organization realizes that 'one option choices' will be rejected by customers.

The organization has to progress to producing 'special' items that are individualized for customers. A democratic approach will allow and encourage this to happen.

Throughout each style, the ability of the visionary is required to maintain employee concentration by communication of the vision. Figure 6.1 shows how the most suitable styles of leadership change according to the quality progress of the organization.

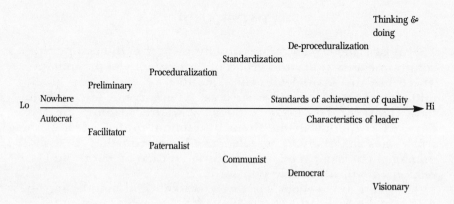

Figure 6.1 Quality leadership style

By recognizing the degree of quality achieved in the organization, an appropriate message and style can be adopted by the leaders. Over a period of time the messages and styles must change to reflect the advancement of attitudes. Sufficient flexibility of response must be tolerated within the organizational structure to allow alternative styles to coexist and to develop from one into the next. This ability to change style is important in large organizations which change at uneven rates across departments.

Over the course of a major project, different parts of the organization will make quality progress at different rates. Care should be taken to ensure that differences of speed within an autonomous unit are minimized and that the slower units never fall more than two steps behind.

Confusion is created if different speeds of implementation are adopted by different sections within the organization concerned. This confusion leads to misunderstanding and means that the speed of advancement of quality performance is limited to below the speed of the slowest sector. Even though the total achievement may be slower than desirable, leaders can use increasing peer pressure to press reluctant staff into changing attitudes.

Chapter 8 discusses strategy in more detail.

Getting the best out of people

For the organization to achieve anything, people must be in place to perform their tasks and functions. Employing the right people is central to the creation of the infrastructure that will generate added value for users. Especially within the finance function, merely providing adequate numbers of employees for customer service is insufficient to ensure that value is added; employees must know what to do, how to perform, and be able to take and implement decisions. In order for the service to be delivered in the best way, employees must have the necessary motivation to perform well. Financial reward alone does not motivate the majority of people to do their job better. The working environment, the freedom to do a job well, recognition of good performance and the knowledge of having done well are all extremely important factors.

On a practical level, for staff to perform at their personal optimum levels three criteria must create and support the motivation of the individual:

☐ Experience — relevant to their position.
☐ Education — knowledge drawn from theories and learning.
☐ Empowerment — to decide and perform.

To increase their willingness and capacity to work, individuals must be developed under each of these headings.

Developing the people

Motivated financial staff will perform their tasks, achieve results, decide priorities and take positive action where the necessary authority has been delegated to them. But unless they are taught and continually encouraged to change and modify their approach, the goods and services that they provide will stagnate. As the organization changes to meet the changing needs of the customer and consumer, so must employees change and improve themselves. In finance functions there have been dramatic changes over the last 15 years, so post-qualification teaching has grown in importance for all professionals.

Ideally, employees should be recruited for their particular experience and relevant education so that they can achieve optimum performance for the firm as early as possible. Optimum performance here is defined as being where ability, knowledge and responsibility are matched to the needs of a position.

These ideas of developing staff can be built into a model to show how development can be managed and directed. Using education, experience and empowerment as framework axes, the personal development paths of employees may be charted to show the relative strengths of the individual. By performing this analysis throughout the organization, a view of organizational needs for resources will be gained. Figure 6.2 shows such a chart.

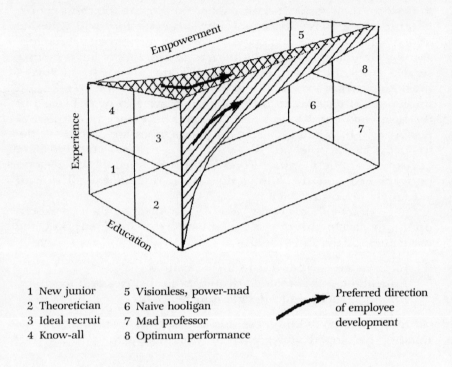

1 New junior	5 Visionless, power-mad
2 Theoretician	6 Naive hooligan
3 Ideal recruit	7 Mad professor
4 Know-all	8 Optimum performance

Preferred direction of employee development

Figure 6.2   The people improvement channel

The rules for using the chart are as follows:

1.   Greater academic knowledge moves a position to the right on the horizontal axis.
2.   Greater experience of a role moves the position higher on the vertical axis.
3.   The less the supervision, the greater is the empowerment.

The chart may be used to describe staff currently in place, so that personal development plans can be constructed to achieve desired objectives, or to address the most effective route to improve new recruits. Resources can be allocated to implement continual improvement under each heading, resulting in the individual being able to operate at optimum effectiveness.

CHANGING BEHAVIOUR PATTERNS

The objective for the business when investing in training and education is to create the desire among staff to change their behaviour voluntarily in order to match new requirements of the company. Companies want employees to demonstrate an awareness of their role so that a greater contribution to profit can be derived.

There are many different methods of attempting to induce behavioural changes, the two most-used techniques being:

☐ the carrot — promises of benefits if change occurs;
☐ the stick — punishment if change is not made.

Neither of these approaches works in the long term. A sensible approach to changing employees behaviour is to recognize two points:

1. The organization exists to serve customers, so an integral part of its objectives must be to learn more about customers and consumers through the experience and learning of its staff.
2. All individuals change their attitudes over periods of time. By helping employees to respond to customers the organization is helping itself to improve and change.
   Internally driven change will always be less painful and traumatic than change imposed from outside.

These points fundamentally oppose the 'Theory X' philosophy which adopts the attitude of never trusting staff, and demonstrate that employees and the company must join together as a team to improve performance. Teams require persuasion, not coercion. By recognizing that staff are an integral part of the goods and services through which value added and therefore profit are derived, the right investment in staff can be encouraged.

Education

Providing education to staff

Providing and encouraging structured learning and training will help employees to understand their role within a department. Employees should also come to recognize how the whole organization operates as a result of the constituent departments providing goods and service internally and externally. The dual aspects of Education are:

☐ Training
   — practical knowledge of tasks that are going to be performed;
   — 'How' work is to be performed.
☐ Learning
   — academic theories, supporting knowledge and understanding;
   — 'Why' tasks are completed.

By acquiring greater knowledge, employees will understand the practicalities of how their role is undertaken. As a result of their training they should be able to modify and improve performance to add greater value for the whole organization. Comprehending the function within its environment will allow them to understand better the needs of their personal customers, and to help them achieve their objectives more effectively.

The importance of continuing education in employment is demonstrated by the recent investment by the government in local Training and Enterprise Councils (TECs). The result of the investment is expected to be the creation of a re-skilled work force, as the need for old skills vanishes.

Training for the role and function

The objective of training is to provide practical assistance and knowledge of the following:

- ☐ Knowledge of what the role is, and how optimum performance can be achieved.
- ☐ Recognition of the authority and responsibility encompassed within the employee's role, and the limitations.
- ☐ Knowledge of the disciplinary systems, and the checks and balances installed to assist the resolution of problems.
- ☐ Basic knowledge about human behaviour, and fundamental interpersonal skills.
- ☐ How the department operates within the whole system.
- ☐ Interdependency between roles within the function.
- ☐ A toolkit of methods and techniques designed to make analysis of performance and improvement of tasks simpler.
- ☐ Ways of simulating experience so that potential methods of improving tasks may be assessed.
- ☐ How different behaviours affect outcomes, and the implications of adopting particular courses of action.
- ☐ Where customers, consumers or users have an impact on the operational aspects of functional duties.

Learning theories of the environment

Academic learning develops in individuals the ability to think clearly and the facility to learn. Training of itself is insufficient for employees as they will not have a framework by which they can understand new experience and adopt totally new techniques. From learning, the following benefits will accrue:

- ☐ An awareness of why the role exists.
- ☐ An understanding of the theories underlying their tasks and role.
- ☐ Why the functional grouping exists.
- ☐ A broad understanding of the whole system of processes, position in local environment, and within society.
- ☐ Expectations of the organization from the individual.

☐ Expectations of the individual from the organization.
☐ Familiarity with the common language, through which common understandings can be reached.
☐ Awareness of the accomplishment and recognition practices operated by the organization.

Some organizations encourage employees to educate themselves continually, helping with the costs and time to do so, even when there is no direct payback to the employer. They do this in the knowledge that education will be undertaken by the individual to add value personally — and if the individual gains, the employer is likely to gain too.

Giving employees experience

Though most people recognize that experience is beneficial when performing a task repetitively, experience only has practical value when the role which is performed adds greater satisfaction for the customer or consumer. As customer needs change over time, so employees have to be provided with the opportunity of providing other services so that their own role may grow and develop.

Learning through experience in the role

The objective of taking action is to produce a desired effect. When individuals experience different and new ways of performing tasks they will notice the effects on their consumers and customers. As more service is given, so the individual gains more knowledge from the responses gained. Listening to requests, complaints and comments helps in a broader under-standing of users' needs.

Understanding the practicalities of different roles allows the recognition and development of standards so that customer expectations may be identified and satisfied. Suggestions to improve delivery in order to meet higher personal and corporate expectations will become oriented towards the practical and achievable.

The personal abilities of staff can be assessed as they perform their tasks so that individual strengths may be highlighted and capitalized upon. Weaknesses may be recognized in the light of real attempts to provide service, and training or education given to resolve difficulties. An important part of learning is the demonstration of knowledge by teaching others. Allowing others to learn from one's own experience is an important consideration when empowering staff — witnessing performance in practical situations can lead to an accurate evaluation of any risks.

Successful sequences in the performance of tasks can be catalogued and repeated, and incorporated in changes to normal practices. Where performance is below the required level, measures to avoid the repetition of sequences that resulted in unsatisfactory outcomes can be implemented.

Communication between peer groups increases the information available for use in the learning and improvement process.

Experience responding to change

Learning through experience should provide opportunities to assess, discuss and make practical improvement in an environment with minimal risk. As change is identified and implemented, mechanisms should be in place to ensure that the right result then happens. This means that the effect of change must be forecast, tested, run through and monitored; it should not be a trial and error system of *ad-hoc* modifications.

The organization can develop a need for change by monitoring how frequently systems and procedures change. The ideas for change can be generated by giving non-specialist work to different or new employees. This will help the organization to keep an open mind when assessing whether a new approach could work successfully.

Empowerment

Empowerment is concerned with the removal of supervision. The concept of removing supervision does not necessarily mean the removal of control; it means the minimization of control. Some organizations embarked on this policy some years ago, and their management structures now show a 30:1 ratio of worker to manager. Senior staff have to manage in these circumstances, not supervise. The old ratio of 7 staff to 1 manager has been replaced, and the span of control argument is seen through new eyes. A 7:1 ratio means that over 14 per cent of total effort is wasted, which can only result in greater expense and less attention to the customer. In finance functions this problem of excessive supervision is frequently much worse than 14 per cent.

Unless and until staff are empowered to take decisions and act upon them, staff are unlikely to accept responsibility for error. Errors and sub-standard actions will result in a lack of quality which will persist until the empowerment route is taken.

Adequate education and experience on the part of the employee are by themselves insufficient to provide an excellent good or service to the customer. Employees must be authorized to act on their own decisions in order to provide customer satisfaction in as short a time as possible.

Trust is central to the empowerment of staff. Unless management display and disseminate trust in their staff, behaviour patterns will not change. From greater trust will spring a new recognition of customer needs and a dramatic improvement from new-found creativity.

Shared trust is the basis of development

When trust is a shared vision between employees and employers, authority is rarely abused. Regrettably, trust between employer and employee in the West is historically rare, as management have never previously recognized the need. Despite this lack of trust passing from senior to junior, high degrees of trust have existed between individuals working in cohesive units within small enclaves of many organizations. These small units are referred to as the 'silos' of function, in which trust between colleagues is common, but rare between departments.

The finance function holds many of the keys to unlocking the waste caused by functional silos, because the technology and systems that can provide the assurance of financial security are now available. If the management wills it, the old fears of theft and fraud within organizations can become a phenomenon of history. Information systems can allay fears of financial mis-appropriation and enable the creation of a new atmosphere in which cross-functional working and mutual trust and respect becomes the norm.

Delegation of the use of power will result in tasks being performed far quicker, as less time will be taken up in waiting.

Recognizing opportunities

A number of respected observers of western companies believe that staff spend the majority of their time satisfying their supervisor rather than the customer or user. Consequently, the general level of quality provided is poor when compared to similar businesses in the Far East. When supervision is removed, staff are able to concentrate on providing service to their customers and users, and can actively seek out new opportunities to provide better or extended services.

Unsatisfactory outcomes can be avoided, because staff will be empowered to take action on the spot. At the other end of the scale, threats to the services from competitors or substitutes will be recognized earlier and addressed by the staff themselves. When all staff understand how to use the quality toolkit the recognition, analysis and decision processes will speed up and become shorter.

Creating improvement

As an environment is created in which staff are encouraged to take action to improve user satisfaction, they learn to take the most appropriate action that they have identified, without waiting for management approval. Management will be satisfied in these situations that the staff have the necessary experience and have been trained to cope with any new eventuality. Thinking members of staff will know when improvement is possible and actively seek out situations in which they may make a greater contribution.

Creating improvement for users will encourage new champions to step forward for new projects. The continuity of the cycle of change will be assured, generated and speeded up if staff see the practical results of their targeted efforts.

KEEPING IN TOUCH — DE LA RUE COMPANY PLC

Background

Turnover £560m. PBT £105m. Net assets £278m.

The largest commercial banknote and security printing company in the world. Activities mainly involve the printing of currencies (banknotes, etc) and security items (cheques, passports), and the manufacture of payment systems (banknote sorters, dispensers etc). Employs over 8,000 people world-wide and over 2,700 in the UK.

Point of view: Group Finance Director

Security is absolutely central to the business of the company; we have to have an approach which simply *is* quality. The attitude in head office finance is relatively simple; as the providers of a service to the board, shareholders and potential shareholders our integrity is critical. Integrity on a much deeper level than one would normally recognize. The full assessment of the consequences of alternatives must be given to decision-makers. Decisions based on finance or other data must not be made in a vacuum. It is up to the finance function to assess the underlying truth of data, and the consequences of possible courses of action.

The history of the function is important. In the 1960s and 1970s, accounting was very much a bookkeeping function only. During the 1970s and 1980s, capital expenditure growth was important and the finance function was under pressure to facilitate this. Now in the 1990s, a measured opinion is required from finance professionals — usually not a yes or no, but advice with an understanding of the real business needs. This requires skilled people, with the intellectual ability to ask the right questions, and to whom the answers will make sense.

With the advent of very powerful micro-computers, there is a danger of data overload for most managers. By using highly skilled and sometimes specialist people, the organization can avoid the production of huge volumes of unnecessary data. In finance we do not have a TQM policy — the clichés have little meaning. Many of our subsidiaries have achieved BS 5750. The whole point about quality in the finance function is that quality is not a procedure. Quality is an attitude.

Top-class people are at the core of quality service provision. To ensure that our subsidiary finance directors are top class, we ensure several things:

1. Top management trust the staff to perform well, allowing for occasional error to facilitate learning.
2. The personal chemistry works well, supporting personal development.
3. An emphasis on personal responsibility for action or inaction.
4. The directors are responsible for the entire function including routine internal control issues, as well as interesting business decisions.

There is a dramatic difference between finance and accounting. Accounting can be formalized into procedures, and be prescribed to a great degree. Finance is about much wider aspects, and cannot be blinkered by procedures.

Guidelines

1. Ensure that all staff add value; employ skills you need.
2. Encourage an atmosphere of trust. React positively to mistakes.
3. Get the attitudes of staff right.
4. Personally assess your staff.
5. Hold regular meetings to keep everyone informed.
6. Use computers properly, to add value.
7. Invest to help the customer.
8. Do not use jargon.

THE EMPLOYMENT CYCLE

As employees progress through their careers, the organization goes through an employment cycle as it selects, employs and develops its staff. Quality principles affect the cycle at all points, and provide the individual and the corporation with the means and understanding to make progressive and positive changes to the many aspects within the cycle.

The stages of the cycle are as follows:

- □ pre-employment;
- □ commencement;
- □ deployment;
- □ development;
- □ retirement.

Other books concerned with human resources cover the implications of some of these topics in detail. In this book, only the main points are extracted and highlighted.

Pre-employment

Before an employee is sought, the avenues of efficiency and effectiveness improvement should first be explored, in order to avoid unnecessary employment. Some of the quality tools could be used to re-engineer and solve problems better rather than simply adding to the pool of resources. The actions to take are:

1. Identify and decide the scale and duration of the needs.
2. Define the specific post by identifying the:
    — skill level, seniority level, expertise, educational standards, qualifications;
    — performance standards and other expectations;
    — personality, characteristics, development potential, disposition;
    — values, beliefs.

3. Initiate the recruitment process:
    — publication of the requirement, which may possibly include briefing an agent;
    — preliminary screening of applicants for suitability;
    — Short listing;
    — assessment of applicant suitability against defined criteria;
    — decision to appoint.
    Employment contract should be issued after agreement with the candidate concerning terms and conditions, etc.

Commencement

☐ Induction within the organization, followed by introduction to the role, function and colleagues.
☐ Basic training for performance of the role.
☐ Instruction and practice of performance.
☐ Priority-setting rules identified.
☐ Management control and reporting methods clarified.
☐ Transfer the organizational pattern of values, beliefs, attitudes for assimilation and take-up.
☐ Explanation of behaviour patterns.
☐ Teach the language common among employees.

Deployment

☐ Assessment and agreement of new objectives and targets.
☐ Performance and practical application of skills and knowledge.
☐ React to attitudes and behaviour.
☐ Communication.
☐ Practical learning.
☐ Role suitability and judgement.
☐ Feedback and improvement routines.

Development

☐ Identify personal and role development needs.
☐ Special training, multi-skilling and re-training.
☐ Responsibility assessment/increases.
☐ Succession and retirement planning.
☐ Discipline.

☐ Alternative roles and approaches.
☐ Training of others.

Retirement

☐ Exit interviews where leaving is not due to retirement.
☐ Service recognition.
☐ Pre-retirement preparation.
☐ Post-retirement care and communication.

Quality initiatives have their greatest impact in the following areas of the employment cycle:

1. Staff numbers

   Ensuring that the fewest possible people are employed to perform the tasks necessary to achieve the objectives of the organization in a sensible way. This does not mean that minimum numbers are employed.

2. Recruitment of the most suitable applicants

   Using quality definitions of the roles and tasks that will be performed, recruitment specialists are able to select the most suitable candidates for employment.

3. Matching employee skills to the needs of the role

   Junior roles are de-skilled prior to automation, senior roles are broadened and thinned to target scarce skills more accurately.

4. Employment satisfaction

   Improved communication and recognition within the company improves morale and motivation among staff. Better user satisfaction and the resulting business decision improvements add up to satisfaction increases for the individual.

5. Employee flexibility

   With more involvement and authority over the decisions concerning their own roles, staff may be encouraged to gain new skills and utilize them in their wider roles.

Where quality attitudes are adopted throughout the organization, the employment cycle itself does not change in any dramatic way, but it is affected by two important factors:

1. Communication

   Staff are kept up to date with important events in the organization and the harmful effects of gossip are avoided Employees discuss and communicate with one another in a common language in order to identify and solve problems, so saving time and avoiding misunderstanding.
   Discussions with customers and users are undertaken with

certain knowledge of the organizational goals and accepted practices, not guesses.

Staff hold similar values and beliefs, so all objectives converge on common beliefs and ideals.

Employees recognize that they all work for the same employer.

2. Recognition

Internal recognition by peer groups, and by the organization itself is enhanced.

External recognition by third parties, by the award of prizes or kite-marks, increases.

Competition can be encouraged with external competitors.

Communication and recognition are probably the two most important factors in keeping a work force 'happy'. They have marked effects on the degree of job satisfaction felt by the employees, and this is likely to reduce staff turnover and increase motivation.

When people are not matched to their roles

Failing to recognize the needs of staff in terms of experience, education and empowerment can cause errors to be made in the promotion of staff and recognition of performance. If we refer back to Figure 6.2, many symptoms visible in the every-day working environment can be explained in terms of their underlying causes:

New Juniors

Employees have insufficient experience and theoretical understanding in comparison with their colleagues. They are not entrusted with responsibility until they prove capability.

Theoreticians

Too much theory creates inadequacies because of the lack of experience of practicalities. A person does not automatically become a good player or team member simply because they understand the rules and procedures.

Know-alls

Experienced employees who believe that they have experienced all possible permutations of problems, and that they are able to provide solutions.

Their lack of theoretical understanding of their surroundings means that when faced with new and extraordinary events, they may adopt inappropriate policies.

At the empowered end of the scale, more dramatic examples of mismatch between role and ability can be illustrated:

Visionless

Promoting know-alls to powerful positions often results in them being perceived as visionless and power-mad. Their view is usually that business will continue much as it has always done in the past. When the changes demanded by the business environment are insignificant, they survive. When changes demanded are momentous, they have no knowledge on which to base their judgement and they fail.

Naive Hooligans

Typically the son of the owner, brought in without experience or learning, who may take decisions having neither the theoretical knowledge of what should result, nor the experience.

Mad Professor

The owner of the company, who has great educational knowledge of theories, fails through having no practical experience of customers.

Identifying where individuals lie within this framework will help the organization to address and make corrections to its policies. Those points at which experience should be offered, training and learning provided, or responsibility and authority given or removed may be recognized and acted upon.

Induction into the company for new employees may be prefaced with an assessment of their status under each of the headings in order to cater for their specific needs. Special attention can be provided to allow them to integrate into the organization in the shortest time possible.

RECRUITMENT — TESCO PLC

Background

With a 1992 turnover of over £7.6 billion, Tesco is a major retailing power in the UK. Profit before property income was £545m. The company has a record of innovation and investment and positively looks for product quality. The company has declared a policy of investment in suppliers, in the skills of staff, in communities, and in systems. Substantial cash amounts are raised annually for charity.

Point of view: Financial control director

The finance function helps the rest of the organization to generate profits by taking a proactive role in the decision-making of the company. Management information is not purely limited to financial data; the potential impact on the rest of the business has to be understood.

The company information systems have got past the stage of making sure the base data is accurate; information systems collect data automatically, which may then be used in reporting immediately.

As a company we are gradually moving away from a paper-based information and reporting system to a screen-based system. This change will place some pressure on the organization to use a higher quality of personnel resources.

Our staff selection standards are already quite stringent for trainee accountants, and are likely to become more so. We generally take in graduates, so their attitudes and behaviours are more important than their history of work.

Practical aspects of training are emphasized through providing a broad exposure to business knowledge. Each individual spends at least three months in at least three different departments. Our policy is to plan individual careers quite carefully.

We benchmark the performance of individuals and departments against identified criteria. Staff and managers then know what to expect, how to improve, and what should be done practically.

Management accounting requires a flexible approach, and the recruitment policy reflects this need. The selection procedures that we use have developed from reviewing the successes and failures of some of our recruits. Psychometric aptitude tests are used for most of the graduate intake. The verbal reasoning and communication abilities of the person are seen to be more important as signals of future success than their numeracy.

Accounting is gradually moving away from the centre toward being physically with the commercial decision-makers. For those in finance the move away from the production of data towards the interpretation of information could become profound over the coming years. This will serve to further emphasize the importance of communications skills for financial specialists.

Commercial managers need access to financial expertise to help make optimum financial decisions. As a consequence we aim to give staff broad experience, train them extensively in interpersonal skills, and help improve general communications. Computers may take out the mechanics from accounting, but machines cannot replace judgement.

Guidelines

1. Improvement must start at the top.
2. Set high standards that reflect the philosophy.
3. Improve communications throughout the organization.
4. Gain company-wide commitment and cascade understanding.
5. The best motivation is from knowing a good job has been done.

WHERE HAVE ALL OF THE FINANCE JOBS GONE?

Over recent years thousands of jobs for financial personnel have vanished. Compared to the late 1970s and early 1980s there are few advertised job vacancies that seek clerical staff. Even allowing for a significant recession in recent years, something more fundamental has been happening in organizations. To try to understand the changes in the jobs' market, a review of the normal career paths of finance staff shows the following:

Level	Information providers	Service providers
1	Junior clerk	Trainees
2	Data controllers	Data input
3	Reporting operators (junior analysts)	Clerical operators (eg credit control, purchase ledger)
4	Providers of specialist information	Data manipulators (forecasting)
5	Business and management accounting	Financial accounting
6	Strategists and decision-makers	Analysts and policy makers

The more qualified and competent the individual, the swifter the rise from junior at levels 1, 2 and 3, to the senior levels of 4 and 5, and on to the director level at 6.

As individuals achieve greater seniority and more financial rewards in terms of salary and perks, numerically fewer individuals can be supported by the business. During the 1960s and 1970s managers used to believe that a ratio of one supervisor to approximately seven workers, and one manager to seven supervisors, created the right hierarchical structures. As automation has blown away massive sections of unskilled work, the ratio of junior to senior staff has worsened and companies have subsequently demanded increased output from fewer of the top-level individuals.

The removal of work from each level can be seen as follows:

☐ Computers have already wiped out most of level 1. Good, small accounting software packages now retail at less than £500.00, and fast personal computers cost less than £1,000. With average clerical finance staff salaries at over ten times the combined total of these amounts, paper-based systems cost substantially more to maintain than computer systems for most organizations.

☐ Level 2 has vanished as more responsibility has been accepted by the individuals responsible for taking action. One implication of the devolvement of responsibility is that staff generate data themselves.

☐ Level 3 is almost wholly automatic, as most computing software already caters for the bulk of customer reporting needs as standard.

The majority of clerical functions can be replaced by computing technology which collects money by direct debit and pays using Bankers Automated Clearing System (BACS).

☐ Level 4 is being replaced by the performance of the users themselves in many instances. There is no need to employ a specialist to provide information if the added value is insignificant, if the work does not take long, or if the work can be completed personally by the user.

In services, progressively more work is being fully automated in that payments are made through direct banking transactions based on goods received notes, not invoices.

☐ Levels 5 and 6 are expanding as more responsibility is devolved to local management levels.

As a result of automation and systems integration, a great deal of routine work has been removed from the finance function. Financial services companies and facilities management companies have targeted low-level repetitive operations and automated them. The result in internal service departments is a heightened need for quality financial skills at lower levels of responsibility, coupled with a reduction in overall financial staff numbers. By introducing mechanical rigour into working practices within an organization, computers are capable of performing all of the financial function low-level roles.

The impact of computing technology

The application of technology and the availability of cheaper computers began to replace mechanical accounting roles and clerical tasks in the 1960s. Since the early 1980s the pace of this change increased noticeably. The phenomenon which is most remarkable is the propensity of organizations to require even more information, a requirement which has grown at an even faster rate than the ability to produce such information. The history of the finance function is one of exactness, of double-checked double entry. The result of such attention to detail has been a reputation for precision and exactness whenever a measure was made or suggested. Because finance and financial measurement has been at the heart of most organizations, a 'quality' reputation has been built up around the accuracy of financial statistics.

A substantial part of the work normally done by the finance function has been to mould data into shape and fit it for use within the organization. As a result of this greater demand for data, and for more interpretation from individuals (accountants), the functions of information and finance have in many companies tended to be controlled by one person. Only in large organizations or technology-based companies have the departments been routinely separated.

The growth of computing technology has been driven by the user requirement to be able to access huge volumes of data quickly and efficiently. The effectiveness of the access has rarely been considered by the specialists supplying hardware and software.

In the vast majority of systems, fundamental access to financial data is gained through the use of the chart of accounts, which is the listing of all possible permutations of all referenced codes to which income and cost may be allocated. Originally, chart of account codes were invariably designed to provide data in standard profit and loss or balance sheet format reports, in which purely financial information was imparted, not volume or statistical data. During code design, the requirements of operational management often took second place to the production of financial reporting information because the priorities dictated by finance have historically taken precedence over almost any other business requirement.

This emphasis on financial information resulted in huge volumes of data being accessible to very few individuals, who were usually based in the finance departments. Centralized decision-making within organizations was made simpler because the concentration of output from mainframe information systems was produced in one place. There is evidence to suggest that decisions are made at the point closest to where relevant information is most readily available, which would explain the tendency toward centralization during the 1970s and 1980s.

During the late 1970s and 1980s information technology matured, and became more than just a service department within finance. Business came to understand that information systems (IS) and information technology (IT) could be used strategically to change the basis of trading in industry, to wipe out competition or to lock in suppliers. Many industries have made massive advances by using IS in this way. Prime examples include international holiday booking, news printing and banking.

On the back of ultra-fast communications hardware, new software-based technologies are facilitating the provision of large volumes of information at remote sites to allow local decision-making. In the last five years, the whole thrust of centralized decision-making has been reversed, decentralization has replaced centralization, and the devolvement of responsibility down to the local operational management has become important. In addition, the operation of advanced technical systems that manipulate data has reduced the amount of time taken to provide managers with the information on which they may base their decisions. With new responsibilities and less time to perform their duties, managers demand more than fast and detailed financial data — they need a thorough information service. Clear examples of this can be seen in any of the recently privatized companies, such as electricity generation and water.

Reliance on mainframe systems for producing information has declined rapidly, as users have been reluctant to wait for the information cycle to be completed. The impact on mainframe computer manufacturers has been highly visible — IBM declared world record losses in 1992.

With micro-computer based systems (often with access to mainframe data tables) users are able to achieve their aims very quickly. What they demand is 'information now to meet my needs'. Although micro-computers are generally very inefficient, they can be very effective. Users decide immediately whether a result is acceptable or not, and whether the time and effort adds value for them.

Mainframe computing power has played an important role in finance. To illustrate this fact, the major clearing banks recently estimated that if their work had to be performed manually, they would have to employ the entire population of the UK to get the work done. In the 1990s micro-computers are bringing mainframe computing power to the desk of operators and managers. Information is available to all through the new and extensive power and communications networks.

Micro-computing

The drive to more and greater local decision-making has been helped by the use of micro-computers. Many complex financial calculations are now relatively simple commands in spreadsheet software — discounted cash flows, internal rates of return, etc. Non-financial staff can now successfully resolve complicated financial questions and operate intricate financial systems.

As new, fourth generation language software uses 'English'-based languages, the need for specialist computer programmers in Cobol, Fortran and Pascal has decreased substantially. As a result of these industry changes, the mythology of computer programming has mostly gone, and with it the delays to obtaining information.

As demonstrated in Figure 6.3 below, the iterative loop involving many specialists to produce mainframe data, has been replaced by much faster and shorter iteration loops that demand personal attention.

With access to many new automated computer functions, the recipients of finance function services and information are able to avoid asking for personal assistance. Significant proportions of these individual users frequently assess the added value of information or service in terms of their own time, ie 'Can I perform the analysis myself? Can I afford the time? Do I have to ask for assistance? Can I afford to wait?'

Where local managers consistently fail to use human financial expertise, the only financial input to their decision will be from a computer. The logical extension of this argument is that these users will demand software sufficiently advanced to replace adequately financial expertise completely. There is no reason to suppose that the software companies will not meet their customers' needs. Professionals must therefore seek to add value in other ways.

Using mainframe data systems

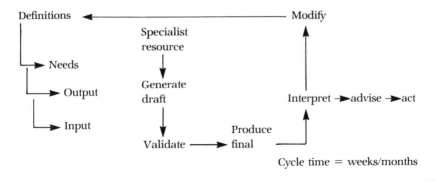

Using micro based data

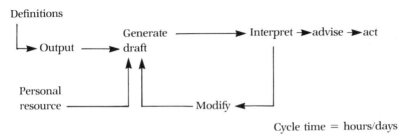

Figure 6.3 The impact of computer technology

Many of the questions asked by users are fundamentally the same as they have always been. However, the assumptions have now changed and the environment for the decisions is moving and changing fast.

The importance of the impact of small, very powerful computers should not be underestimated. Information systems have been having a major effect on the demand for information for over 20 years. Only now in the 1990s have computers fallen in price sufficiently for individuals to consider them disposable items.

Over the next 10 to 20 years, computer industry observers suggest that computing power will increase, and size and cost will decrease, with the result that computing will become a personal possibility. Access to massive amounts of data will be swift, easy and cheap, and as systems grow the ease of access will improve.

The implications of these changes are that there will be less and less demand for finance functions to act as data gatherers, and there will be an extensive replacement of specialist skill with specialist software systems.

COMMUNICATION

Financial figures are a medium of interpretation, a language through which diverse demands and requests may be understood in common terms. Over a long period of time, financial language has grown complex and difficult to understand. As a result of this complexity and unfamiliarity, many users of financial information believe that financial terminology has been designed to mislead and irritate. They fail to understand debits and credits, debtors and cash flow statements. In spite of being employed to provide interpretation, many accountants are notoriously bad at communicating information. Perhaps this failure is the reason why many executives have historically chosen to 'shoot the messenger' when finance personnel bring bad news.

Communication is a critical skill to the finance function. Good communication transfers essential financial skills to users which they may then apply in the performance of their duties. Good communication is two-way — receiving and transmitting — and is primarily visual and aural. Two aspects are important:

☐   how effectively the transfer of knowledge is completed;
☐   whether the manner of communication is acceptable.

Perhaps the most important reason for the misunderstanding of the finance function and its motives is the lack of discrimination on the part of users and stakeholders between the cause of a bad result and its effect:

☐   The effect of poor credit control is high work in progress.
☐   The cause of poor credit control is likely to be the result of poor sales techniques, poor sales management, poor clerical performance, poor communication with the customer, and poor credit control techniques.
☐   The effect of poor management information is poor management decision-making and sub-optimal priorities for the staff.
☐   The cause of poor management information could stem from inaccurate assumptions, base data, presentation, environment, poor systems or bad management.

The finance function reports information and progress over which it may have no direct control itself. When losses are declared or the financial results do not meet expectations, the effect is that finance is seen to report the bad news caused by the actions of other functions. Although finance may have contributed to the problem by providing insufficient information to management, the cause is rarely within the finance function. Only from applying better communications will stakeholders and users recognize the real causes of problem and error, and take action to correct them.

7

Numerical Issues

PLACING VALUES ON THE PROBLEMS

Most organizations do not value the cost of failure; they value only the costs of inputs and attempt to match these costs to sales' values. The whole accountancy profession has been oriented towards accounting for total costs within a time period, and then summarizing these costs into a profit and loss account. Neither historical nor current cost accounting values unnecessary failure within the organization; they only measure costs within a period of time. By placing all costs into boxes that only relate to the point at which expenditure was incurred, every performance of every individual is averaged out and neither the best nor the worst is singled out for special treatment. This is a case of mediocre systems providing mediocre results.

Quality principles suggest that by measuring the cost of conformance to specification within the organization, both the best and the worst may be identified. To do this, the criteria for conformance to specification within finance must be clearly defined and measured. Given their current systems, this kind of measurement is not a possibility for most organizations.

Until quality measures which can recognize conformance are developed for the finance function, the alternative is to take the opposite approach and to define the criteria of non-conformance. Staff are usually much more able to say if a service fails to deliver to expectations than to state whether the service actually fulfilled expectations. By identifying when service fails, it is possible to conclude that all other service must have been successful (a dangerous but unavoidable assumption), and only measure the costs of non-conformance (CONC).

The reader should beware of the difference between unauthorized cost and unacceptable cost. Unauthorized cost is the result of error, fraud or theft. Unacceptable cost is the result of sub-standard performance of service or product arising from a process. Historically, finance functions have successfully ensured that no unauthorized cost is incurred — these costs are usually less than 1 per cent of revenues. Unacceptable costs have been largely ignored, and are frequently estimated at between 10 per cent and 30 per cent of total revenues.

Cost of conformance

When the organization produces a unit of perfect output in the shortest possible time at the lowest possible cost, the cost associated with that unit of production is the cost of conformance. Costs of non-conformance are any other costs.

In essence, satisfactory expenditure needs no explanation. Where the organization collects and reports on data, it has no need to know the details of any satisfactory expenditure. For this reason, the vast majority of reports that are produced within organizations are quite unnecessary.

The concept of unacceptable costs (as opposed to unauthorized costs) depends upon the clear definition of 'conformance specification, testing and acceptance', and the mutual understanding of these between the parties concerned. For a service to conform, the practical result or output of the process must pass the acceptance tests of quality of service output. If output fails against these quality criteria, such output is non-conforming and the associated costs are costs of non-conformance.

For example, where a financial specialist is required to produce a special report, the cost of conformance is the 'first time' value of time, materials and services consumed in completing the following tasks:

☐ Planning where and how to get data.
☐ Designing the method by which the report will be produced.
☐ Collecting all of the basic data, if it is readily available and accurate.
☐ Checking that all relevant environmental information is included.
☐ Producing the report.
☐ Ensuring the user understands the output, and is able and trained in how to use the information.

Identifying the costs of conformance can be extremely difficult, and the costs can themselves be misleading. One important difficulty with measuring conformance is that over a period of time the quality measurement criteria should change as user expectations increase or staff abilities improve. Continually improving the base level of quality acceptance testing is an accepted part of the quality process.

A simpler approach is to teach staff how to recognize and measure waste.

Cost of non-conformance

Because waste is neither measured nor monitored within most finance functions, there is major cause for concern that costs of non-conformance are out of control. Most companies admit to CONC being between 10 and 15 per cent of their total costs, though they do not normally monitor the costs in normal accounting reports. Manufacturers can measure CONC much more easily than service companies because their products are visible and may be inspected relatively easily. CONC in finance functions will generally be much higher than in a manufacturing environment, and has been observed at levels of over 50 per cent. Within CONC, three main types of cost have been identified. These are the costs of:

☐ prevention;
☐ appraisal;
☐ failure.

Within each heading, two types of financial values are feasible:

1. *Actual costs* — incurred as measurable expenditure. For example:
   — internal — added costs or values since processing started;
   — external — original and additional third party costs;
   — appraisal — value of time and materials of assessment;
   — inspection — value of time and materials of extra/additional checking;
   — verification — cost of double-checking work completed and passed;
   — prevention — extra cost of early use of resources to avoid later failures.
2. *Opportunity costs* — the cost of not doing something, valuation subject to opinion. For example:
   — revenue — lost sales;
   — skills — sub-optimal use of specialist resources available;
   — non-personal resources — finance, equipment, skills, etc;
   — time — potential losses of revenues and profits.

To simplify the difficulties of measuring the costs of non-conformance, a service organization may value those events and actions that add no positive value to the output of the organization. Usually, CONC costs detract from the value of the organization either directly (by incurring a cost paid to a third party), or indirectly (where time that would otherwise be used to generate revenue is used ineffectively).

To test the level of one's own CONC:

The identifiable tasks performed in an average month should be listed, and the average number of man-hours spent on each noted against the headings. This will normally provide a reasonable estimate of how between 70 and 90 per cent of time was spent at work. The difference between the actual time accounted for and the total time available is the 'unidentified CONC'. Analyzing the work content further will show a further percentage to have been unnecessary or wasted, which is the 'identified CONC'.

In a report produced by the DTI in 1992, the costs of quality

(COQ) were generally believed to be between 5 and 25 per cent in UK companies. COQ is often unmeasured and therefore uncontrolled, though by measuring it organizations will take action to improve performance against the new criteria. Definitions of conformance can change — depending on the user — and time measurement is complex and difficult. As a large proportion of quality is based on self-assessment, gathering information about CONC is initially more about guesswork than science.

The DTI cites the example of British Aerospace dynamics division, which had 11 per cent of total costs recognized as COQ. Half of the amount related directly to the cost of failures.

To correct quality problems within BAe, a strategy was adopted of:

☐ defining and clarifying the purpose and strategy of the quality initiative;
☐ reporting only figures produced by the finance department;
☐ using only validated standard information;
☐ improvement, starting with failure costs and progressing to appraisal and prevention.

It follows from this that costs were allocated to codes which grouped values based upon whether the outcome was desirable, and not whether the cost merely related to the identified title of a profit and loss account. By separating costs based on acceptance criteria, and not account coding criteria, two implications logically follow:

1. Errors are valued, and made visible to all concerned.
2. The apparent link between cost price and sales price is removed.

Both of these represent major benefits to most companies and organizations in that:

☐ processes and people that add net value are highlighted so that action may be taken to improve financial performance;
☐ the sales price is based on the amount of added value to the user as a result of the product or service. Pricing is not a result of the cost incurred by the provider.

Within the finance function the costs of non-conformance usually have to include some implied costs and values resulting from the process applied. For example, there is no simple way of deciding how much added value is created by paying suppliers on time. An element of false benefit is incorporated by introducing the opportunity cost that could result if the process is not undertaken, but this is unavoidable.

For example, if there was no credit control department, most debtors would pay approximately 60 days late (say). This increases working capital and interest costs. More importantly, the delayed payment reduces the availability of funding for growth, which may have a significant value.

A value for services may be implied by taking expected investment interest rates, growth factors, dividend rates, and risk percentages into the calculation. Implied values should be checked against third party external supply costs; for example, make a comparison between in-house credit control costs and the cost of factoring debts.

The cost of failing

The primary aspects of failure costs identified by academics are:

1. *Direct failure costs*
    As quality of output increases (services or goods or information), the costs associated with failure will fall.
2. *Appraisal costs*
    Appraisal costs are relatively fixed as the entire output must be appraised. As quality increases there may be opportunity to lower total appraisal cost from simplification of design and performance.
3. *Prevention costs*
    By forecasting and solving problems in advance of incurring failure costs, total costs of quality will decline.

In recent years the mathematics behind the cost of failure has changed dramatically, as illustrated in Figure 7.1. Where very high quality was previously believed to incur very high costs, it is now believed that the higher the quality the lower the overall cost. This argument is justified on the basis that quality is a definable set of criteria for any good or service and the total cost of quality is related to failing to meet those criteria.

For example, this means that the costs of quality for a Ford Sierra can be directly compared with the costs of quality for a Jaguar — both have different levels of quality defined within them, but both can have measures of how well they achieve their different criteria.

If we look at the modern view illustrated in Figure 7.1 we can see that the total costs of failure can be minimized by:

1. Increasing the frequency of feedback, which minimizes direct unit failure costs. This is because more feedback causes faster improvement and shifts the whole graph to the left.
2. Achieving improvements to fundamental quality levels. This will lower the height of the costs of failure curve.
3. Preventing failures, in order to appraise less. This will reduce the minimum level of costs incurred in appraisal by temporarily increasing the costs of prevention. The appraisal curve is a straight line, whereas prevention costs are curved.

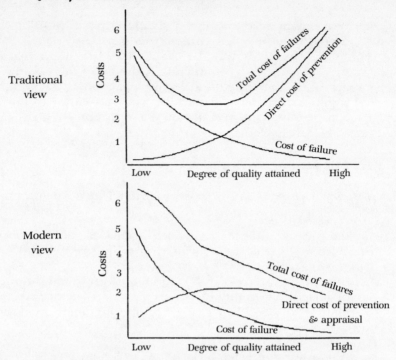

Figure 7.1   Costs of failure: traditional vs modern views

QUALITY MEASUREMENT

Measurement is only important in that it represents a change or a scale of change in the subject being monitored. One should not be deceived by a surprising measurement into believing that the measurement itself is important — only the relationship of the measurement to its context is actually important.

The primary means of controlling the output of any system is by measurement of actual achievement against expectation. Though measurement is central to the role of finance, few quality measures within the function itself are routinely taken and reported on.

Quality measurement requires the skills of attending to detail normally found within the finance function. Also required are the skills of system design, data collection, presentation and interpretation. These developed skills now need to be turned upon the function itself in order to recognize what should be measured, reported and improved.

Two kinds of measurement of quality achievement may be taken:

1.   The success or failure of an operation — where true or false type answers may be sought.
2.   The relative degree of success or failure achieved — where

opinions and perceptions can be ranked or graded against known criteria.

These measures do not relate to the costs and resources consumed, but to the result of the delivery or process. As with all measurement, the importance of the measure is in the generation of a trend and in deciding upon the necessary action to be taken to correct or improve the position.

For those that wish to measure CONC in a service organization, policies concerning where, what, and how measurement is taken should be communicated to interested parties. Here we address the subject under the following headings:

☐ Subject boundaries.
☐ Practical quality measures.
☐ Representing quality in monetary values.

Subject boundaries

Measurement against quality criteria is best performed at the limits of jurisdiction of authority, across a perimeter where ownership or responsibility transfers from one party to another. At these boundaries output is either accepted or rejected according to acceptance criteria or custom and practice. Individual people are usually held responsible at these points and who may take corrective action where necessary.

If problems are allowed to pass through boundaries unchallenged, blame shuffles between the sections (these organizations invariably allocate blame) because the culprit is both the creator of the problem and the recipient who failed to spot the problem. The consequence of allocating blame is that staff concentrate on fire-fighting today's problems rather than making ready for tomorrow's opportunities.

When taking measurement, the broad horizon must first be defined so that the part of the organization to be assessed is clearly understood. Measurement can take place at different levels, depending upon whether a strategic, tactical or operational perspective is being taken.

To better meet the objectives of the organization, measurements will be required to evaluate performance on the following planes:

☐ The organization within its surrounding environment.
☐ The organization alone.
☐ A specific subsidiary or division.
☐ In a department.
☐ For the individual.

Within the boundaries of each section the inputs, business processes and outputs must be clearly recognized. Through this process of identifying resources and consumption, the section itself will be clearly defined, and the basis of quality control will have begun. Where resources enter into the section's system, the acceptance criteria have already been defined in contractual terms. To improve quality substantially, many companies simply need to gauge and monitor their acceptance criteria slightly differently. For example, in a hotel, do not measure food supplies by total weight received, measure the usable weight received. In a component assembly plant, only measure supplier failures at final test stage. Prohibit suppliers from supplying parts that do not work.

When a section is delivering products or services to an internal or external user the same kind of rules apply, except that they are extended to include management items. For example:

☐ In a printing factory, measure how much paper was extracted for being below quality specification before product finishing.
☐ Measure the period taken to develop a new service from conceptualization to first delivery.
☐ In an accountants' office, measure how long the processing time was for purchase invoices.

The classification of organizational boundaries and selection of key parts of the transformation process also helps to identify cost drivers for use in activity based costing (ABC). Under ABC, the principle of reporting costs according to the fundamental cause of the cost applies equally to service, manufacturing or public organizations.

Where to take measurement

The simplest way of controlling an organization financially is to control at its perimeter. By controlling physical inputs to and physical outputs from an organization, one will completely and effectively control the organization. This is because the only other variable factors affecting output are those of time and management. This principle of control at the boundary is sometimes known as 'perimeter fencing'.

To develop this principle further, the best points at which to take quality measurements are always at the start or finish of responsibility for the subject under investigation. This could be the point of ordering of incoming items, or the point of despatch for outgoing items. For transfers within the organization itself, the easiest point of control at which measurement can be taken is usually where a good or service is either:

1. transferred to a new owner;
2. consumed.

These principles may be applied to an individual, a department, or to a whole organization. Many organizations make the mistake of only measuring at the point of transformation of the input into an output. Measurements taken at the point of transformation are only useful within financial accounts, as such measurements are historical. They are irrelevant because they have not asked such fundamental questions as:

1. Do you want this?
2. Now?
3. In this volume?
4. Does this meet your specification?
5. Was the specification correct?

Some organizations use mapping to help them decide where to measure quality, and which criteria must be measured.

In Figure 7.2, the control points are those at which service or product ownership is passed to the customer. These are the points at which measurement should occur. The points must be reviewed regularly to decide whether the criteria for quality should be changed.

Figure 7.2 shows a map of an organization involved in providing specialist sub-contract labour against large contracts. The main processes which add value for customers are the points at which some measurement should occur. Inverted triangles depict the points where decisions are made and rectangles the points where other events occur. The figure highlights those points at which measurement is essential because of the direct relationship with the customers. Similar maps can be drawn for any organization to show the points at which measurement should be taken. To minimize the amount of data and work required to control the organization, measurement should be concentrated upon the critical points.

Actions taken within the finance function should relate directly to the main processes of the organization. When reviewing the events occurring within finance to decide whether a measurement is required, a measure must be specified if the process is critical to the organization.

What should be measured

At the point of measurement many things may be of general importance to the management of the organization, though rarely are there more than four items of significant importance. Commonly, only two items are reckoned to be of critical importance.

If measurement is made in monetary values, great care must be taken concerning the method of data collection, because successful delivery does not mean that a successful conclusion has been reached for the customer — one does not necessarily follow from the other. The fact that a customer has paid an invoice does not necessarily mean that they will return to purchase more goods or services.

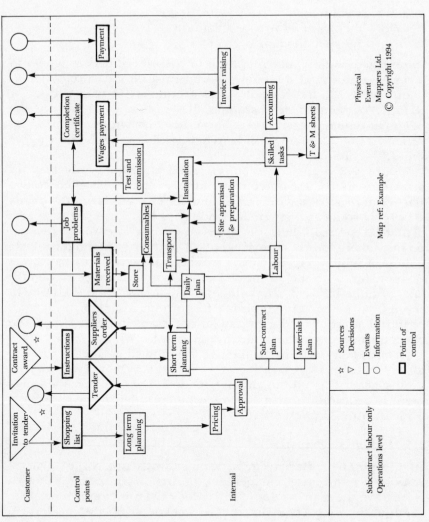

Figure 7.2 Business process mapping example

There are no hard and fast rules for deciding what would be the best quality criteria at a control point, though the persons responsible for providing the service at the point of delivery are invariably the best people to consult to identify what should be measured. Quality measures should change from time to time, because once one particular problem has been solved, another of a slightly different nature may be expected to arise.

Many organizations take some measurement at critical points, but usually of a monetary value only. Rarely are measurements of customer perceptions taken at these points. For example:

☐ Superstore till sales are measured in £ sterling, but no measurement is taken of repeat business from customers.
☐ Hotels measure the amount paid to suppliers for foodstuffs, but fail to measure how much in volume or value of the products was actually usable.

To measure quality, most organizations have to collect data relating to completely different criteria than those on which they normally report. This is especially true for the measurement of success for finance functions. Some finance functions measure their success based on the number of days taken to produce accounts, rather than how up to date those figures actually are. It is false economy to produce numbers within four working days of the month end when most of the figures consist of poorly estimated accruals. Others measure success from the number of computer print-outs distributed to managers within the organization, without regard to accuracy, timeliness or relevance. Such measures are blatantly useless. Local finance experts must develop sensible measures of quality with their users, and then manage their systems and techniques to improve total satisfaction.

A great deal of quality monitoring is self-assessment so the atmosphere within the organization must be one of mutual trust and recognition. Blame for problems and retribution for mistakes should not be distributed among staff and management. At the simplest level, blame adds no value.

When developing measures remember that the finance function has special needs:

☐ The organizational measures must have a customer/consumer focus.
☐ Finance function measurements must have a multi-user focus.

Practical quality measures

Many accounting and financial systems measure and report on the valuation of items. Few systems measure how well the task was performed. It is this qualitative opinion that must be sought and reported. Within finance, many specific measurements may be taken to monitor the speed, efficiency and effectiveness with which the operation is undertaken.

The main parameters for measurement are:

- time/date;
- total volumes;
- errors;
- user usage.

Each of these may be expanded to show more qualitative and quantitative data. Some suggestions are listed below.

Elementary level

Measures here rely upon statistically based data that may easily be gathered, eg:

- The time actually taken compared to that expected.
- Days spent on *ad hoc* reporting.
- Days wasted on unnecessary work.
- Total volumes throughput compared to expectation.
- Total number of errors compared to volume throughput.
- Exception reports versus standard reports percentage.
- Whether reports were actually used by user.
- Number of user training days undertaken.

The units of measurement frequently indicate the degree of advancement of quality within the organization:

- Percentages — not started, or recent starter.
- PPT (parts per thousand) — advanced quality initiative.
- PPM (part per million) — world class performance.

Intermediate level

Organizations that progress to this level have normally adopted some degree of real quality into their operating systems, and have achieved genuine results. The measures outlined below begin to address issues that are less dependent upon hard facts and evidence, and highlight the importance of the use of time and multi-dimensions of performance:

- The date action was taken, compared to the earliest possible date of action.
- Total time spent correcting errors.
- Post-project analysis — data, information, environment, decision.
- Assessment of training provided against required.
- Customer opinions.
- Supplier opinions.

Advanced

Few organizations have moved forward to measure and monitor user perceptions of financial services offered. Examples of what should be done include:

☐ Assessment of the added value of preparation and production of data and information.
☐ Improvements against benchmarked standards.
☐ Degree, volume and success of improvements achieved this period.
☐ Shareholder, general public awareness polls.
☐ Management analysis of decision optimization.
☐ Customer poll of credit control approaches.
☐ Appraisal of payment systems by suppliers.

Many more examples of possible items to measure could be listed, but they tend to be industry specific. Readers should think about how they could apply this approach to their own situation.

Representing quality in monetary values

As we have seen in earlier, translating problems and failures into monetary value is rarely straightforward. An important point to consider is whether financial representation is necessary at all. In many cases a financial valuation is not essential to measurement, and in others the valuation could detract from the overall qualitative benefits. If the organization wishes to represent quality and failures in financial terms, valuation falls into one of three categories:

1. **Externally charged**
   This is where additional external quality costs incurred are the subject of a third party invoice. The values can be identified separately and reported on relatively easily. These are the most common costs associated with failure simply because they are usually easy to see. They are also usually the smallest cost.
2. **Internally incurred**
   This is where intra-company transfer pricing passes added cost or added value between sections in the organization. To calculate the value of failure, the processes or criteria within the specification which add value or add cost must be defined.
   An inconsistent or potentially unfair approach will result in either conflict or sub-optimal decisions as managers sub-contract to third parties rather than use under-utilized internal resources.
   Finance functions frequently charge fixed costs for their services, which itself fails to reward users for improving their own use of the services.

3. **Opportunity costs**

These costs are representative of the value of time and resources if they had been used differently. The value is not expended, it simply evaluates what might have been.

Introducing imaginary costs into profit statements is always dangerous, as lower-level managers may be deceived into believing that their 'opportunity profits' can be converted into cash.

If opportunity cost is included, a policy must be adopted to ensure consistent treatment across the whole organization. This policy must declare how 'imputed' costs must be calculated and shown, and whether they may be compared with actual costs. Targets may be set for the imputed costs in the same way as for actual costs.

The calculation of imputed cost can become quite intricate. For instance, if the monthly accounts are produced one day late, the impact is less severe than their production ten days late. The likelihood of extra cost being incurred as a result of reporting ten days late is quite small, but the chance of a late decision adversely affecting the future costs of the organization is relatively high. Business losses resulting from the lack of timely decisions are the likely consequence of a poor financial information department.

One possibility for valuing information departments is to treat them as an insurance item, working on a percentage of the opportunity cost savings and/or potential profits or losses.

USING TECHNIQUES — ELEY LTD

Background

A subsidiary of IMI PLC, employing 140 staff with a turnover of approximately £10m. The main product is 0.22mm sporting ammunition bullets produced to very high quality specifications. The company also manufactures most of the specialist packaging that it requires. Exports account for about 80 per cent of production. The company was certified as conforming to BS 5750 standard late in 1993.

Point of view: Chief Accountant and Company Secretary

The company started the TQM approach several years ago, and management then were not very receptive to the sometimes radical ideas for change. The new management do seek quality, and follow the principles of continuous quality improvement. Quality is a key point in the mission statement, and is reflected in our actions.

As a matter of course, our operational managers do use statistical process Control (SPC) to quite an extensive degree. This level of control has produced substantial financial benefit for the company.

We are developing the TQM culture so as to devolve responsibility down to a personal level. This also means that *ad hoc* reporting systems and patterns are becoming very much more structured. In practice the senior managers go through fine details with staff until basic information is correct, and check that the priorities and timetables have been set. The personalizing of the company mission statement is now being considered.

The company is a member of the local business network through the Engineering Employers Federation, where ideas are swapped and benchmarks compared between members. This is a useful umbrella organization against which our progress can be measured.

As a company, we are now looking at generating more and better information concerning costs of quality, or costs of non-conformance. The fundamental problem is that one must not allow subjectivity to enter financial reports. Financial information at the lowest levels must either be accurate or not produced at all.

Some of the arguments for CONC are a little esoteric, perhaps because no reliable method has yet been found for measuring good management. For an organization to improve, it must have a measure against which success may be gauged. CONC figures should be a simple way of evaluating costs differently.

As a company we are more interested in marginal cost than how overheads are apportioned. We have considered ABC and found it unsuitable as a basis for either price setting or decision-making for our type of operation.

Guidelines

1. Employing the right people is essential.
2. Engendering the right attitudes is equally important.
3. Operate good systems. Plan events and then work to the plan.
4. People must know what to do. Train them.
5. Have a mechanism for gaining an overview of the business.
6. Inspect less. Exception report more.

Pitfalls

The change in attitude toward procedures is interesting. Although procedures have imposed some discipline on previously 'undisciplined' staff, they have not added value directly.

Make certain that quality initiatives always have management backing. If management are unable to see the programme benefits, do not expect the staff to improve.

The problem with counting

The first problem that arises when money is counted is that one has to be very careful to define 'money' clearly. On a macro-economic scale the Chancellor of the Exchequer uses many 'M' figures, eg M0 is the amount of printed cash and bills in circulation. The problem of defining money for companies and working organizations is equally difficult.

Money is a medium of exchange which can be counted, logged, graphed, monitored and even traded. More than this, money is a facility that can change from minute to minute or hour to hour. Because it is easily lost or stolen, finance functions have attempted to control money very tightly. In the UK and US especially, a great deal of emphasis has been placed on the completeness, accuracy and definition of financial statements. Industries have grown up around the control of the data and information needs of stakeholders in every organization. Auditors have developed specialist techniques, procedures and practices to arrive at a series of judgements concerning the numbers in published statements and their underlying systems.

Until recently accounting professionals and many non-accounting professionals jumped to the conclusion that both the results and the methods of accounting are 'quality'. Because they believed the figures unreservedly, individuals and corporations made investment decisions. Users of information failed to take account of the different points at which money can be monitored, and the adverse effect on data reliability that time creates.

To help in the counting and measuring of money, care must be taken to ensure that the user is aware of the different levels at which value can be measured. These levels are:

□ commitment accounting;
□ cash accounting;
□ historical accounting;
□ current accounting.

Each method of counting values a potential or actual transaction at a value that takes account of the period of time between the taking of the measurement and the actual cash transfer. Consequently, each method incorporates degrees of inaccuracy.

The organization must choose the most suitable level of measurement for its own purposes and apply those policies consistently. Users must be educated to recognize the level of measurement, shown in Figure 7.3 below, as poor comprehension can lead to serious misunderstandings.

Commitment reporting includes assessment of 'final out-turn' costs, or estimated costs to completion. Cash reporting tends to avoid the concept of accruals and the spreading of expenditure over several periods, and has real problems with capital expenditure. Historical methods analyze revenue and cost, and attempt to define the precise total of transactions that occurred subject to adjustment for stock, accruals and prepayments. Current cost reports adjust the imperfect historical reports to account for the change in the underlying buying power of the currency itself.

For many years, very large organizations have tended to measure at the earliest stages of expenditure for financial accounting and publication purposes, while cash measurement

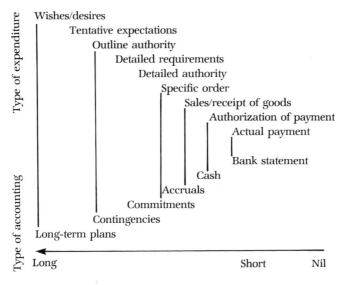

Figure 7.3 The monitoring of money

has taken precedence for management reporting (eg the National Health Service and British Rail). Each of the large industries has built up its own set of accounting policies which treat transactions slightly differently. This has led to the employment of analysts working on the Stock Exchange who specialize in the interpretation of numbers provided by the companies.

In spite of their specific accuracy, financial numbers may be generally misleading because the greater the distance between measurement and the actual cash value transfer, the less likely the measurement is to be exact. Though an estimate of future cost may be precise to the nearest £1,000 at the time of estimate, the final cost could be millions different from the actual when it is incurred. The Channel Tunnel building costs are an example of this phenomenon. Even when specific orders are valued prior to invoicing by the supplier, values can easily be inaccurate by more than 10 per cent, which could be more than the profit involved on the project. Current cost accounting attempts to resolve the problem of elapsed time by adjusting reported values, historical accounting fails to measure the impact of inflation, while cash accounting neglects to recognize all the transactions relating to the current time period.

Recognizing where financial measurement is made assists in the development of techniques aimed at addressing discrepancies caused by those measurements. The main causes of discrepancy between reported figures include:

☐ Pre-transaction
  — Processing delays, omissions, undiscovered errors;
  — value of time and the cost of borrowing;
  — competition and unforeseeable occurrences;
  — risk.
☐ During the transaction
  — timing;
  — valuation;
  — fraud, theft.
☐ Post-transaction
  — inflation;
  — misallocation;
  — changes in preferences/perceptions;
  — omissions, undiscovered errors;
  — residual valuations.

Discrepancy between financial numbers is also caused by the application of the matching concept. Under normal accounting conventions, revenue is declared in the time period in which the sale occurs. Product costs are matched to the items sold through the stock accounts, and expenses are matched to time through the use of accrual and prepayment accounts and the profit and loss account.

For evaluation purposes, the finance function must decide the point at which revenue is generated, and whether incurred costs relate to revenue or to time. As a general guide, costs are matched as follows:

Costs matched to Revenue: Products, cost of goods sold; contracted work that directly relates to a sale.

Costs matched to time: Expenses; work that cannot be related to a sale or asset; undefined services.

For example, in a credit control department that manages and recovers debts for two divisions, charges are made on a percentage of the divisional sales turnover. The organization must decide whether bad debt recovery costs are part of the direct cost of sales (and so could increase WIP), or whether they are overhead expenses.

Discrepancy is also caused by applying the prudence concept too literally. Under the guise of being prudent, costs are overestimated and revenue is underestimated. All of this discussion serves to underline the fact that the measurement itself is not important. The context of the information and the trend of change of the resulting statistics is, however, of the utmost importance.

And, of course, the difference in treatment between reporting for taxation purposes and accounting for commercial judgement adds another dimension to the issue of what should be reported.

UNDERSTANDING YOUR BUSINESS — NATIONAL GRID COMPANY PLC

Background

Turnover £1.4bn. 1993 current cost profit £310m. Current cost fixed assets £5bn.

Before privatization in 1989 the company was a part of the Central Electricity Generating Board (CEGB). From the CEGB, the generators, the Grid and 12 regional electricity supply companies (RECs) were formed. The RECs retail power to users, National Power, PowerGen and Nuclear Electric are the energy producers, and the National Grid transmits all high voltage energy between them. The Grid is mostly owned by the RECs, and is also responsible for the pricing of electricity through the 'pool' system.

Point of view: General Manager Finance

National Grid Company history is one of engineering excellence, limited by bureaucratic and political control. Only since becoming the largest PLC electricity transmission business in the world have we been mostly free of political control. The impact on our accounting has been enormous. Before privatization there was no such thing as profit, there was only a 'return on assets'. The formula was this:

Costs + Return = Income.

Costs and return were known items; income became simple mathematics. Arguments used to be back to front. In the early days we really had to work at getting the understanding across that income was actually dependent upon customers. It sometimes felt like an 'Alice in the Looking Glass' world of fantasy.

Since privatization we have been emphasizing, through many different initiatives, the importance of quality at all levels in the organization. There is still a long way to go.

Our adopted philosophy is one that allows the managers of the operating units to choose whichever quality route that they wish. Unless they 'own' the process, it will fail. This philosophy also allows for different speeds of achievement without causing too many problems for the rest of the organization.

A quality initiative has to have a rationale, or purpose; being merely 'a good idea' is not sufficient justification for making significant investment.

We have spent a long time just making sure that the objectives of the organization were clearly understood. Within this, the most significant part was the recognition of the customer and their inherent importance to the business. We used numerous business games to help our management understand the issues. Our staff are very highly skilled, and it was important that they understood the approach we adopted. We are taking a blueprint approach to quality in the organization. This entails focusing on the characteristics required, defining them, and then providing solutions using known technology in a manner that will allow practical implementation.

The concept of quality is a much misunderstood path. This can be illustrated by a proverb:

It is easier to convert to a new religion, than to start believing.

Guidelines

1. Keep patience. Do not expect everything to happen overnight.
2. Change the orientation of the organization on to the customer.
3. Keep the whole organization in step where possible.
4. Obtain good advice.
5. Monitor results and make adjustment where required.

Useful tips

Use benchmarking to ensure that your organization is improving at least as fast as any competition. As a minimum, compare your cost structure to that of your opposition.

We have reviewed activity based costing (ABC) methodologies but the technique has not yet developed far enough for our requirements. It can help address the problems of effectiveness, but it has real problems in addressing efficiency.

Process re-engineering may help the self-improvement mechanism.

At the end of any project the positive aspects and learning points should be emphasized, not the failed aspects. This is because any later initiative could be made far more difficult due to a lack of enthusiasm, or fear of failure.

Always remember, quality is in the eye of the beholder.

CAPACITY AND QUALITY

Capacity is initiated by demand, made possible through resources, and brought into being through action. Quality affects the speed and effectiveness of actions taken by individuals, and so may increase both the potential capacity and the achieved throughput for no extra cost.

Capacity is the volume of units of output expressed per period of time that the system can produce at its maximum speed of throughput while still meeting customer requirements.

Service system capacity is constrained by four factors:

1. The availability of customers.
2. The availability of resources (people, machinery, supplies, time) to transform inputs into outputs and effect delivery.
3. The volume of output produced which does not meet acceptance criteria.
4. The cycle time for the processes.

In a service industry or department, every person represents an individual process or a series of processes; people are the equivalent of machinery in a manufacturing plant. A service organization has bottleneck people in exactly the same way that manufacturing industry has bottleneck plant and machinery. Quality addresses all of these four constraints directly and allows the organization to improve and increase total service capacity. First we must define what total service capacity actually is in generic terms.

The maximum capacity of a service system is equal to:

$$\frac{\text{Process time available}}{\text{Unit process time required}} \times \text{utilization}$$

Process time available is the time available to the individual after breaks, and may be specific to the time of day, month or year, depending upon circumstances of the individual.

Unit process time required is the total time spent at the process for each work unit requiring that process. In services, work units often require flexible or unequal timing, and so each should be treated individually. The time includes set-up, delivery, clean-up and learning time.

Utilization represents the expected percentage of time that may be used effectively according to the differences caused by user requirements. For example, Day 1, received 8 requests at 60-minute intervals throughout the day, each request taking 30 minutes to resolve — full day utilization = 50%; Day 2, received 8 requests at 9 am, each taking 30 minutes to resolve — half day utilization = 100%

Capacity output in finance functions — indeed in any service function — often suffers from very high peaks and very low troughs of demand for service or information. This phenomenon is frequently referred to as the 'boom or bust' syndrome. Successful management of the highs and lows is made more difficult as capacity restrictions vary according to the day and date, and the skills of the personnel involved. Examples are most evident at budget preparation time, month end, or during the production of the year end accounts.

To avoid an unacceptable distribution of work load, any of four alternative capacity policies could be adopted:

1. Increase the availability of processes by increasing personnel. This does not improve efficiency or effectiveness, but adds unused potential capacity.
2. Reduce the processing time for the work unit. Using volume measurement criteria, efficiency will be increased.
3. Increase utilization by managing the flow of work. Steadying the flow of work will increase efficiency by minimizing resource inputs.
4. Reduce the total amount of work required. Increases in effectiveness result from avoiding unnecessary work. Many

measurement systems are unable to discriminate between efficiency and effectiveness.

The capacity of small staff numbers to perform time-consuming operations like month end accounts, accruals and consolidations has been dramatically increased by the use of computers. The mundane preparatory work for both information and services has been largely removed through automation. The production of accounts for large companies can be fully automated to produce sales and purchase ledgers and all profit and loss accounts in final form within hours of the close of business. Instead of major projects occurring at specific and usually inconvenient times of year, work can be spread over the whole year, thus smoothing out the flow of work. Demands for greater volume throughput in finance has led to the replacement of labour-intensive operations by computing power which uses machines that can read, machines that can sign cheques, and financial systems that do not need any paperwork at all.

Demands for greater uniqueness of service have led the finance function into areas previously believed unnecessary if not impossible: revised budgets every month; forecasts by the day and week; detailed sensitivity analyses of many 'what-if' options where the future is uncertain; international trading in financial instruments on a massive scale; and, from financial creativity, the birth of new multi million pound markets.

The importance of time

In a service environment, time is money. Indeed, some academics believe that time is everything and that all values could be expressed terms of time and not cash. Time may be bought and sold, and traded and manipulated in the same ways as any service commodity, but time cannot be physically moved. The management problems caused by this are huge, because time appears to get shorter the nearer that the due time comes. The staff costs within a business are all related to the time that staff spend performing tasks, and the total time that an asset may last defines the likely cost of using that asset.

To simplify the analysis of the problems caused by time, it can be defined in six ways:

1.	**Total time**	The total volume of time potentially available to the employers of the employees' time. For example, for most employees this is the eight hours per day that they are on site and available for work.
2.	**System time**	The time spent in which performance of work can be identified. For example, for the individual, system

		time is the amount of time working on identified tasks that can be accounted for.
3.	**Wasted time**	There are two types of wasted time:
		— Identified: known tasks that were unnecessary.
		— Unidentified: the difference between system time and total time.
4.	**Cycle time**	The time taken for a normal unit of work to pass through the processing system from input to output. For example, the time taken between the request and final delivery of a special report for management is, say, six days. The cycle time is therefore six days.
5.	**Processing Time**	The amount of time that is spent actually processing work units through the system. For example, the special report that took six days to deliver required a total of eight hours of work for a financial expert and two hours of un-manned printing. The processing time was eight hours.
6.	**Lost time**	The difference between cycle time and processing time. For example, for the management report in 4) and 5) above, the lost time is five days assuming that one day equates to eight hours' work.

Quality techniques apply to time in two ways:

1. Obliterate any wasted or lost time.
2. Optimize all system and processing time.

Manufacturing organizations seek to reduce and minimize the amount of time allocated to system and processing time; for service organizations the same rule does not apply. The service requirement is to satisfy the customer and the degree of satisfaction will not necessarily increase if the period of time allowed is shorter.

Processing time can be reduced by training and thus improving the abilities of providers and users so that misunderstandings are avoided and common understandings are reached. By standardizing inputs to the system, the pressure on data entry might be eased significantly. For advanced companies, intelligently flexing the system may avoid the need for any standardization.

Time management techniques are not new. Most auditing accountants and major-league management consultancy employees monitor their time to the nearest 15 minutes. These organizations understand that time in a service organization is critical and can be charged to the client because value is added as time is consumed.

Special considerations for system time

System time is the name given to the amount of time that is consumed by individuals working to support the provision of a service. System time is all time spent on identified work, including the setting of deadlines, arrangement of routines, the specification of running times for tasks, the allocation of times to groups of tasks, and the time taken to perform specified duties.

Figure 7.4 shows an example matrix of how time and work interact and how the analysis of time can show surprising results. Unidentified waste time in finance functions is frequently as high as 30–40 per cent. This is caused by interruptions, extended meetings, phone calls, etc. Part of this waste is caused by the effect of troughs in work load at certain points in a period, when there is little work to perform.

The percentages shown in Figure 7.4 are illustrative and are not meant to show either good or poor practice. The value of the percentages is irrelevant; only the rate of improvement matters.

Time analysis for: Mr John Smith   Month: Jan 94

			Total potential working time	100%		
	System time		50%–90			Unidentified wasted time
Identified tasks	Planning	Set-up	Performance	Clean-up	Identified wasted time	
Quarterly accounts	40%	20%	30%	10%	30%	
Credit control	10%	50%	20%	20%	45%	
A/c payable	10%	30%	30%	30%	25%	10%–50%
Monthly accounts	20%	10%	60%	10%	30%	
Special reports	30%	30%	30%	10%	40%	
Average	22%	28%	34%	16%	34%	

Figure 7.4 Analysis of total working time available

Strategies

REASONS FOR A STRATEGY FOR QUALITY IN FINANCE

To create an atmosphere which develops quality in a logical and consistent sequence, a strategy must be formulated and implemented which will affect all staff — from the most junior to the most senior — in terms of what work is done and how work is done.

The benefit of declaring a strategy is primarily that the organization will be able to see and understand where it is heading and why. Employees then have an opportunity to act in concert and start making progress towards the stated objectives by modifying their actions earlier than would otherwise be possible. Without a declared strategy or a series of policies, new training initiatives, new experience opportunities and new staff empowerment procedures will be treated with cynicism. Most organizations have procedures and policies that relate to quality in finance, but rarely could these attempts be recognized as a strategy.

The absence of a strategy to achieve financial quality is most frequently demonstrated by many organizations' lack of certainty that they employ the right number and grade of personnel in their finance functions. This uncertainty is often accompanied by the statement that 'with more people we could do more work'. This comment reveals that any value added by the support function to the core services of the business has not been recognized within the support section concerned. For finance, the root cause of these problems is that finance staff numbers have almost always been justified by the statement 'we need these people', which has rendered most output and performance measures irrelevant.

Management can, and frequently do, discuss quality. They may become committed to its principles but it is the staff who must be persuaded. Although the ideas and drive may start at the top and work down, practical change has to occur at the bottom and work upwards.

A strategy is the basis of effective communication between colleagues in the finance function. Initiatives taken without an overall strategy will run into apathy within the organization and be lost.

A STRATEGY FOR BUSINESS EXCELLENCE — RANK XEROX

Background

During the 1970s and early 1980s the main markets for the company were being attacked by Japanese industry with great success. Rank Xerox was one of many companies that suffered loss of market share, revenue losses and shareholder value loss, in addition to job losses.

As a result of its adoption of quality principles, Rank Xerox has been able to rebuild market share, based on a wider business strategy.

Outstanding performance and the achievement of high quality standards throughout the company was recognized in 1992 by the award of the first European Quality Award.

Point of view: Quality manager, finance and business process and information management

Quality has been the central building block of the company for over ten years. Without this change in emphasis the company could not have survived the competitive onslaught.

By improving everything — from the smallest components of products to staff attitudes — the company has fully recovered its competitive position.

Positive customer opinion and perceptions build up over a long period of time. If a company suffers from a loss of customer credibility it takes a lot of time for the company to recover. Quality is the means of changing customer perceptions and cannot be switched on and off at will. Quality is a long-term strategy.

The company responded to the dramatic changes in the photocopying and printing market by recognizing that achievement of business excellence is a necessity for the future. We encapsulate the concepts under six main headings:

- [ ] management leadership
- [ ] Customer focus
- [ ] Human resource management
- [ ] Process management
- [ ] Quality support and tools
- [ ] Business priorities and results

Self-assessment against these categories and their composite criteria is central to our management process and to our annual objective setting process.

To sharpen the edge of leadership through quality and as the basis for ongoing business improvement review, the concept of Business Excellence Awards was introduced. This is an internal recognition of continuous improvement in standards of service in all six categories.

Resulting from the assessment process is a list of actions, which are the few things which must occur for the continuous or breakthrough improvement to be achieved. They range from simple modifications to complex organization-changing requirements. The policy deployment or objective setting process which follows distils the action plan into a set of 'vital few' key actions. The policy deployment process cascades these vital few actions down to the individual level so that all members of staff are able to see how their own objectives support the company.

Changing the culture of the organization has taken more than ten years, and we are still changing. Because the concepts of quality are not new to the company, all the staff now understand the quality language and jargon, have similar values, and understand and use the same tools and processes for defining and making improvement.

Quality has to be an all-pervasive belief. The programme must be ongoing.

There are two objectives in the improvement programme:

1. To identify breakthrough ideas for process management.
2. To generate across-the-board efficiency increases continuously.

The tools that staff use play an important part in the continuous improvement process, ranging from simple fishbone diagrams to complex process re-engineering charts.

All of the staff are trained to use and apply the techniques to identify and implement improvements. On average more than four days are spent teaching the seven statistical tools, the management tools, other essential frameworks, and getting across the message that improvement is a personal responsibility.

The company makes extensive use of benchmarking, which can be performance, process or product related. Quantified measures of performance are classified under quality, cost, delivery and value.

Both internal and external comparisons result in judgements being made concerning where best to make improvements. The process is both cyclical and continuous.

Guidelines

1. TQM must be an overall strategy, not just finance and IT.
2. Top management must lead the initiative.
3. Focus on the customer — this can change business priorities.
3. Create enthusiasm, generate ownership; people are the key.
5. Obtain personal commitments.

DIFFERENT STRATEGIES FOR APPROACHING QUALITY IN FINANCE

The strategy that best suits the organization is a function of the style of the organization, its culture, and the attitudes and beliefs of influential managers and directors. The starting point for the organization and the volume of work that has to be completed also have a significant bearing on the choice and speed of direction.

Depending upon the attitude towards change within the organization, one of four alternative strategies may be adopted to introduce and achieve quality in the finance function:

1. **Financial vision**

   Least cost, highest quality, best environment, highest added value, best decision-making, organization driving.

   Company-wide initiatives drive through change and build on success.

2. **Piggy-back**

   Least cost, highest quality, best environment.

   Company-wide initiatives primarily aimed at lowering costs through education and experience. Low cost is seen as important, but not at the expense of reducing revenues.

3. **Me too**

   Least cost emphasis.

   Applying to specific departments, based around peer group comparison. Concentration on cost reduction rather than added value.

4. **Topic based**

   Least cost emphasis.

   Applying to specific sectors, possibly within departments, based around peer group comparisons in which individuals 'go it alone'. Concentrating on cost rather than added value.

The best option to choose will also depend upon the degree of maturity of the quality vision within the finance function itself compared to the level of understanding of quality within the entire organization. The more advanced the management thinking, the more embracing the chosen strategy is likely to be.

Each alternative is equally valid and will achieve practical improvement in proportion to the resources allocated to the task. Within each option, leaders may choose from a range of paths to achievement, depending upon either an adversarial resolution to problems (we can do it better than them) or the development of compromise solutions (we can solve it better together). The relative success of these divergent choices may depend upon the degree of conflict between the staff and the leaders, and the speed of improvement necessary within the business.

At the lower levels of strategy, the potential for conflict between senior management and staff is significant because of the desire of management to adopt faster speeds of implementation than the employees are able to cope with. Conflict is not necessarily an evil; managed positively, it is beneficial.

Where organizational culture and leadership style both operate to achieve the same end at the same speed, there is little internal conflict because the individuals who make decisions and implement actions are in agreement.

By selecting the most appropriate strategic approach to the implementation of quality in finance, the potential for negative conflict will be minimized and the conversion rate of potential benefits into actual benefits will be improved.

BEHAVIOURAL ASPECTS OF A STRATEGY

The result required from the implementation of a strategy is noticeable behaviour and attitude changes. From a commitment to quality principles staff will modify their approach to work as a whole, and will change the way in which they communicate and interact with their peers, superiors and subordinates.

Personnel must be affected in terms of:

☐ what they say;
☐ what they think;
☐ what they do.

In order to change behaviour and attitudes, staff must:

☐ all understand the same language;
☐ achieve a common understanding of problems;
☐ use common tools to solve and prioritize problems, and implement solutions;
☐ continue to develop and improve their personal attitude and behaviour;
☐ willingly share commitment to the methodology;
☐ be shown how quality affects everything that they do;
☐ practically exercise the learned techniques;
☐ receive the necessary support from the organization.

One should first discover whether staff are likely to be in favour of the process of change. By categorizing individuals as leaders, champions, operators or facilitators, specific training programmes may be targeted at sections within the company to provide maximum benefit. Understanding the orientation of individuals will allow the adoption of plans to minimize the potential for conflict as changes are implemented, and the targeting of resources to minimize costs.

The four categories can be described as follows:

Leaders are those who understand and believe the vision, act in multifunctional roles and provide encouragement and ideas.
Champions are practical decision-makers who seek to take action aimed at encouraging the peer group and subordinates to take similar action.
Operators form the majority. They perform actions under guidance or act in concert with others.
Facilitators are those who are unable to perform a role that requires practical action but encourage and persuade others to take action (eg senior managers, directors, consultants).

Changing the behaviour of employees can take huge amounts of time — and therefore energy and resources. At the heart of the strategic decision lies the issue of timing, because the speed of implementation and the adoption of new quality methods and new measurement techniques is central to the issue of success. The organization must be able to adopt the behavioural aspects of quality safely and at its own pace. If the speed of change is too fast, the practicalities of the operations will not change at the fundamental level, and the hoped-for achievements will not materialize.

Positioning the people

Another use for the normal curve is to explain the attitude of individuals in terms of willingness to take on new approaches and behave in new ways. 'Leaders and laggards' is the marketing term normally given to groupings of customers. The principles of categorizing market sectors according to their speed and willingness to respond to change applies equally to individuals. Figure 8.1 illustrates this.

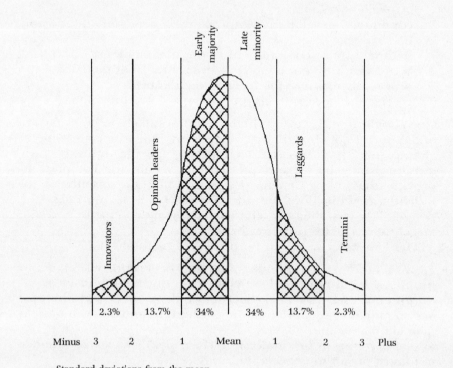

Figure 8.1 Positioning the people — leaders and laggards

Innovators within the organization are likely to have been persuaded to the quality vision long before the directors took up the cause. These individuals normally welcome change.

Opinion leaders may be most suitable for roles as champions because they represent forward thinkers among their peer group.

The majorities — early and late — characterize the bulk of the operators, some preferring modest change, others preferring little change. Good leadership and clear explanation is required to persuade these of the quality vision. Once converted they will need continual assistance, but will make practical improvements where required.

Laggards will only be persuaded when they can touch, see, hear and feel results. Their cynicism takes some time to overcome, especially if they become 'terrorists' but they can be shown how to understand that the changes have helped everyone — including themselves.

The termini are unlikely ever to be converted to the quality vision, regardless of the facts that are put before them, unless they are put into the situation where they absolutely have to try something new. When these people are 'converted' they become the stalwarts of the new ways, and can be brilliant exponents of the methods.

THE SPEED OF CHANGE

Every organization has its own routine speed of change that has been developed over a period of many years. This routine speed is a function of management ability and vision, staff willingness to change, and the environmental pressures for change. Some organizations prefer to take the approach of 'we will get there — one day', while others prefer to take positive steps to respond within defined time-frames to achieve their goals.

As companies make incremental improvements and change their orientation, the speed of change is dictated by the speed of learning of the staff and their readiness to progress to the next incremental stage. All large organizations change in an incremental fashion, building small successes and demolishing failures, so that the whole organization improves step by step. History shows that the more successful the change within a section, the greater the growth of that section, which leads to greater power and promotion for the individuals. Ralph Halpern, for example, generated major success in Top Man and was quickly promoted within Burtons.

This process of incremental change encourages the evolution of the organization and its development is founded upon previous success. Achieving success is crucial to development because without measurable success a project will not survive. Success must be measured in terms of operational improvement, progress must be valued, and rates of achievement must be monitored against target.

The approaches taken by organizations to the concept of quality have been identified as:

1. **We will get there — eventually**

    This option is chosen by those that have more pressing needs than quality. Other, perhaps more crucial, points may be addressed, such as survival, profitability, borrowings and customer loss.

    Even though most business experience suggests that without quality the organization will fail, there is a small chance that success will be achieved through the ordinary efforts of management and staff.

    If there is no objective or measure, there can be no progress.

2. **We set targets and monitor progress**

    By setting and monitoring targets, some attention at least will be paid to the ideals of genuine effectiveness and cost reductions.

    In a rapidly changing environment, when all the attention of management must be on the content of the task, quality may be pushed to the back of the queue.

    For many organizations this is a sensible place to start because from here the steps to real improvement are relatively short.

3. **Continuous improvement in all we do**

    By repeatedly taking action based on good information concerning the operational aspects of the work content, continuous improvement will result.

    Because management and staff understand and believe in quality, a commitment to change is generated which results in change becoming an opportunity, not a threat.

Each approach indicates a different commitment to quality.

STRATEGY FOR QUALITY IN FINANCE — BOC GROUP PLC

Background

The BOC Group had a turnover of over £2.8bn in 1992, split one-third Europe and Africa, one-third the Americas, and one-third Asia and the Pacific.

Total operating profits were over £410m from the divisions of gases, health and vacuum technology.

Point of view: Group Finance Director

The quality concepts that the company espouses are directed at making prioritized, global improvements. To achieve our aim of continuous improvement, we first published a statement of corporate vision and values. This was to ensure that we understood the words and that our staff then understood us.

The cornerstones of the ideals and thoughts are:

☐ integrity;
☐ employees;
☐ competencies;

☐ the desire to 'live' TQM;
☐ globalization;

and management philosophy, technology, safety and communications.

This represents the framework within which decisions are taken. To an outsider, some of these may seem to be motivated by something other than profit. This observation is correct.

With an understanding of the corporate vision, the QiP (quality improvement process) takes over the practicalities. This initiative operates throughout the group and applies equally to finance. The five essentials of the process are:

☐ Consistently meeting customer expectations.
☐ Measurement of customer satisfaction indicators.
☐ 100 per cent conformance to expectations.
☐ Error prevention through improvement — less waste on correction.
☐ Management led by commitment.

The improvement for the finance function was started here at the centre, because top-level commitment must be visible from the outset. To translate the words into deeds, we set up a series of quality improvement projects running under the auspices of quality improvement teams. Teams are set up with objectives, measures and timetables within which they decide and specify any action to be taken. All corporate teams have senior managers (usually directors) as their sponsor and operate to short timetables — usually between three and six months.

Projects are cross-functional and include items such as information management, appraisals, business awareness and corporate centre vision.

The publication and promotion of teams' findings and results are central to the success of the role, so we have regular updates printed and distributed. Annual conferences play an important role in getting the messages across.

Newsletters, conferences and prize givings form an important part of the communications within the group. They are used to keep people informed of progress and to re-emphasize the messages, recognize achievement and demonstrate top management support for the initiatives.

Guidelines

1. Learn the terminology, and research before starting.
2. If management are not convinced of benefit, stop and train them.
3. Make quality a way of life.
4. Use extensive communications as part of the programme.
5. Encourage local initiatives. Be flexible.

TARGETING IMPROVEMENT

Converting from a position of weakness to a position of relative strength cannot be accomplished overnight; the organization must be shown the path and it must be one that produces some early success. A sensible strategy is one which is formulated in order to produce the greatest benefit in the shortest period, with the minimum of risk and lowest cost. By targeting specific areas for improvement, both the speed and the cost-benefit can be maximized.

There are two ways of deciding priorities: taking a general consensus or an evaluated analysis.

The point of making improvement is to have an effect. This entails (in the parlance of Rank Xerox) taking the 'vital few actions'. By analyzing all of the options and ranking them according to priorities, those that represent the best opportunities will be identified. Doing this will define the level of resources required, the speed of response necessary and the likely benefits.

The reason for this ordering of potential actions is so that the actions most likely to achieve success will be performed first.

In order of importance, priorities are usually grouped in terms of:

☐ easiest benefit;
☐ quickest benefit;
☐ largest payback;
☐ least risk of failure;
☐ least impact of failure.

The effect of leaders and laggards among the staff means that early success is important in reinforcing the new quality messages. Innovators must bring the early majority to 'conversion', and the late majority must be persuaded by success to convert.

By scheduling the more difficult achievements to take place later in the programme, the probability of success is increased. Success breeds success, continual success generates an expectation of success, and failure disheartens.

The early decisions on prioritization should be made between targeting resources towards the operations in either the front room, near the customer, or the back office.

Analyzing risk/reward options will be simplified by the examination of specific services to show where maximum operational or financial benefits will be generated from any proposed change. After the target services have been identified, the work cycle should be dissected in the following way to generate ideas for improvement:

☐ feedback;
☐ evolve;
☐ develop;
☐ create;
☐ deliver.

Roles may then be allocated to individual personnel to clarify and ensure:

- definition of the measures to be used;
- data collection modes;
- responsibility for identified processes;
- responsibility for action;
- time-scales and schedules.

TARGETING THE IMPROVEMENTS — NATWEST INSURANCE SERVICES

Background

A wholly owned subsidiary of National Westminster Bank which was significantly enlarged by acquisition in 1991. The company provides advice on life insurance, pensions, investment business and a range of corporate and personal insurances.

Point of view: Service Quality Manager

NWIS has been putting a lot of effort into continuously improving the quality of the service we offer to our customers. The impressive changes brought about by our quality service action teams illustrate the success achieved.

As a result of taking measurements against standards, a great deal of work has been completed concerning items such as document turn-round times, phone call answering, etc. The company has achieved substantial improvement and now distributes the results of performance monitoring to the branch network.

Two years ago we undertook a total quality management programme, which helped further with our objectives in improving quality, but we now feel that more attention must be given to many of the issues on the softer side of customer service — empathy, responsiveness, assurance and reliability.

The finance function has been looking specifically at ways of moving toward greater customer focus by taking on several initiatives:

- Improving communication between departments.
- Empowering staff to make changes and provide solutions.
- Staff development and training.

This process was started by sending a questionnaire to internal customers, asking for comment on performance and for areas to be identified which required more urgent attention.

The result of this is that regular liaison meetings are now held, in which open and constructive dialogue takes place and solutions are found.

GETTING FEEDBACK FROM THE USERS

Once the users or customers have been identified, the starting point for defining any service or information provision is the question:

- 'What do you want?'

When the service is being developed or improved, the question may become:

☐ 'How should it be different?'

Both of these questions seek feedback from the user so that an assessment or improvement programme can be begun. Even though these questions are so fundamental that they seem foolish, many finance functions have failed to ask them.

The questions themselves may be asked through many different channels. These channels include:

☐ the provider of the service;
☐ representatives;
☐ specialist advisers;
☐ multi-user groups;
☐ committees;
☐ user representatives;
☐ surrogate(s);
☐ questionnaires;
☐ returnable documentation.

Feedback resulting from questions will be in either written or verbal form. The most important point about feedback is that it should be understandable and that potential for improvement can be identified. In the instances where the user or customer is not available to answer questions, service providers are well advised to ask themselves the questions on behalf of the actual user(s) and to act as a surrogate user.

The manner in which questions are asked is also important because sympathetic criticism can be very constructive and false praise extremely destructive. Those that ask the questions must be aware of their crucial role in the cycle of improvement, and should communicate with the users at a later time to notify them of action taken as a result of the feedback.

Attitudes adopted by users usually reflect the attitude taken by enquirers; the response to a constructive attitude will often be a helpful reply from the user. Confrontation and criticism should be avoided.

GETTING FEEDBACK — HOSKYNS

Background

Hoskyns Group is a computer services company that was taken into European private ownership in 1992. The company employs more than 3,300 people, has revenues in excess of £190m and profits of approximately £10m.

The information systems management sector (facilities management) and project management account for 80 per cent of turnover. There are four main operating divisions and up to 200 profit centres which act with a great degree of autonomy.

Point of view: Senior Finance Manager

The finance function acts primarily as a support to the rest of the business, helping with planning, getting the back room things done, and providing information and advice.

Many business areas are certified to ISO 9000 standard but that has really been only part of the move into quality. As most of the company's operations directly interface with customers, quality has always been and will continue to be an essential aspect of our work.

In the field, the company assesses quality with the customer at regular intervals. This principle is translated into the finance function in very practical ways — we also sit down with our customers, ie the business managers, and discuss the service, information and personal support that is provided. Many of the business managers have become very interested in the process because they realize that they are directly paying for our services through the inter-unit charges. Charges are apportioned between our customers and reflect the level of support we give.

Standard information produced is quite detailed for each profit centre, including such things as profit and loss statements, variance analyses, and six-month rolling forecasts. However, it is through the provision of *ad hoc* reports and assistance that a real value added service is provided by the finance function.

In order to assess our service and plan to improve quality we began by using informal groupings to discuss what we did well and what could be improved. From this we determined that we really did need to understand our customers' requirements.

To identify our customers' perceptions, we sent them a questionnaire, asking them to grade the services that they received from the different sections in finance — management accounts, purchase ledger, sales ledger, etc. We also asked what their expectations were, and what level of service they really needed.

There were some very interesting answers. Finance had a lower opinion of themselves than the customers, and a much higher expectation of the level of service that they should provide. We are now using this information to plan and implement a programme of improvement, part of which will involve training courses on customer relations.

Once the company actually knows what level of financial expertise is required by the users, resources can be matched to needs. After all, there is little benefit to be gained from providing a 'Rolls-Royce' service when a 'Cavalier' equivalent is what the business managers really want.

Guidelines

1. Identify your own quality criteria, compare this to your customers'.
2. Recognize whether you are satisfying your own or your customers' needs.

3. Involve external users when making decisions.
4. Always seek more and better decision alternatives.
5. Get customer approval for any changes.
6. Never stand still, strive to improve continuously.

EVOLUTION, DEVELOPING FINANCIAL FUNCTIONS — DESIGN

Financial experts often spend a great deal of time designing systems to produce information for users, and consequently their own systems design receives less attention. Many difficulties arise because financial systems are designed to be used by financial operators but the practical application of the system lies with other users. A mismatch between functional design and operator ignorance has frequently resulted in systems that provide numerical accuracy, but commercial irrelevance. Examples of this include: sales ledger systems that do not interface with either sales order processing or stock systems, and purchase ledger systems that fail to monitor unit volumes.

Applying quality principles to the evolution and development of finance function systems will avoid sub-optimal results. The process of evolving and developing the procedures and processes for financial information and financial service needs is outlined in Figure 8.2.

The objective of the design and improvement of a process is to simplify the achievement of value added for the user.

Object oriented programming systems (OOPS) for computers has been developed in recent years, in which the objective of the resulting programme is to provide users with what they require in the shortest possible time and, in the most easily understood manner. This frequently means that the machine does long and complex operations in order to arrive at a simple screen result. The programming technique has developed as a result of recognizing users more accurately and answering their needs and wants more directly. Converting the OOPS methodology for use in designing financial systems goes back to original quality criteria and means:

☐ Keep basic data simple — avoid holding duplicate data-sets.
☐ Update environmental information constantly.
☐ Simplify reporting for users — aid the understanding.

Other important factors are:

☐ Who designs? Match the ability of personnel provided to the need for skill within the project.
☐ What for? Always keep the users' objectives uppermost in mind.
☐ When to be produced? Timing is often critically important to

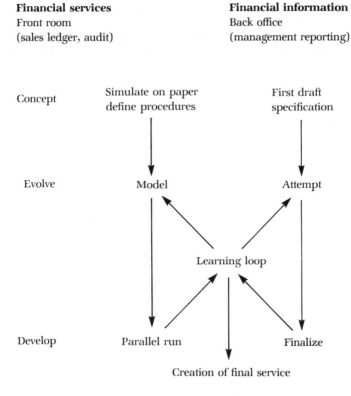

Figure 8.2   Finance service evolution loop

the design of financial systems. Infrastructure requirements may demand special knowledge and consideration.

An irony of design within the finance function is that the greater the pressure of deadlines and immediacy of work to be completed, the less time is available to perform the planning that may alleviate the pressure of work. Every increase in work load should be met by increases in the planning, monitoring and control of work load.

DELIVERY — PROVIDING THE SERVICE

'Ideal perfection is not the true basis of English legislation. We look at the attainable; we look at the practical'
W E Gladstone 1809–98

This sensible declaration of belief in the setting of realistic objectives and targets is one that we all could learn from. In many instances, perfection is the enemy of progress because the time that is lost waiting for the extra improvement is lost for ever. No amount of service perfection can regain lost time.

When the service is finally delivered to the consumer, it represents the fruition of all the strategies and training, all the planning and background work, and all the responsibility, experience and empowerment. Making the most of the short time in which delivery occurs is crucial, so *aide-memoires* have been developed to help staff perform their roles better. An example is the following:

Concentrate
On time
As required
Listen
Think
Improve
Keep learning, listening and helping.

Another example of a company using various means to stimulate its operators into changing their behaviour is the tale of the American haulage company that wanted to improve the appearance and demeanour of its drivers. Mirrors were placed on the inside of the doors of the wash-room toilets that would be used by the drivers. Printed in bold letters on the mirrors was the phrase 'You are the only representative of the company that our customers ever meet.'

DESIGNING AND RE-DESIGNING SYSTEMS — NATIONAL GRID COMPANY

Background

National transmission divisions are broken down into areas responsible for local supplies. The transmission system involves moving energy from generators on to the grid, keeping the grid charged and then passing power to the users. Measurements are taken at all points of transfer.

Very high value assets are in use and depreciation costs far outstrip labour repair and maintenance costs.

Point of view: Area Accountant and Business Manager

Accounting for the area is extremely complex, simply because of the plethora of demands that users make upon us. Local junior management need information based around their personal responsibilities, local senior managers require differently formatted data, head office requires different information from division, and the Regulator requires information in a completely different way. Then, of course, there is also the Inland Revenue and Customs and Excise.

The Grid has been in the process of making major changes to philosophy in recent years and this has made the whole basis of our data less certain than it should ideally be.

Recently, finance has become much more important in the context of investment and repair and maintenance decisions in the company. This has affected overall quality, in that costs are now the result of 'fitness for purpose' rather than an engineering desire to increase the expected life of an asset.

The finance approach to quality that we have adopted at area level entails identifying data in its smallest constituent part, ensuring that the coding and other data is correct, and then allowing the computer systems to provide summaries for information purposes. By this method, the figures 'try to get to what is real'.

Unless the base data makes sense, and the required information gets to the right people, the financial staff are wasting their time advising others on how to interpret the numbers.

Unless the lowest level of data is under control, there is no control. Control of account coding is among the most basic of the tasks of the financial staff, but it is the most important. Quality of basic data is something that we are striving for and will soon achieve.

Guidelines

1. Get the raw data right.
2. Control data at the lowest level.
3. Review systems to decide how best to operate.
4. Enthuse and motivate staff by involving them.
5. Work to very tight reporting timetables.
6. Financial accounts should be the same as management accounts.
7. Communicate all the time.

Pitfalls

1. Some staff prefer job protection to business process improvement.
2. Poor communication.
3. Do not monitor how well the forecasting works, look at the business.
4. Management of details, rather than the big picture.
5. Lack of feedback from the users of information.

Comment

One area that many people overlook is the chart of accounts. The chart can be the method of avoiding massive amounts of work later in the development of the organization. The chart must be set up flexibly in the first place, after having listened to the managers that will use the information. Large and unnecessary amounts of extra work will then be avoided.

If the organization operates many different information systems, careful attention should be paid to integrating them properly. Do not allow continual 'patches' to cover up errors and omissions. Work-arounds cost time and money.

9

Toolkit

USING A QUALITY TOOLKIT

There are numerous techniques that may be used by individuals and organizations to further the development of quality. These techniques are usually referred to as quality tools. By consciously recognizing and training staff in the use of quality tools, problems and issues will be identified, addressed and resolved more quickly than would otherwise be possible.

Human knowledge and understanding do not suddenly appear as if a light were switched on. Progress is of a cyclical nature and can be speeded up by applying appropriate techniques. The techniques should be included in the materials taught to staff. When significant organizational change is contemplated, all staff must have reached similar understandings of the problems simultaneously.

The cycle of understanding and resolving problems involves:

☐ identification of problems;
☐ problem analysis;
☐ option generation;
☐ selection of preferred solution;
☐ implementation;
☐ evaluation.

Within each phase of the cycle, quality tools provide varying degrees of assistance so that common understanding and common resolutions may be reached. Figure 9.1 shows the main kinds of quality tool, arranged to show the main strength of the tool in terms of:

☐ external views, showing if and how external considerations affect its use;
☐ internal views, showing whether it is used predominantly for internal purposes;
☐ environmental assessments, where the tool helps to identify or recognize non-process items and criteria.

The figure also shows whether the tool is based on statistical information.

Each of the tools is defined and described below.

Name of tool Primarily used with:	External	Internal	Environment	Statistics
Added value analysis		☆	☆	
Benchmarking	☆	☆	☆	
Cost benefit analysis	☆		☆	☆
Critical path analysis		☆	☆	☆
Failure mode and effect analysis	☆		☆	☆
Fishbone, cause/effect, fault tree		☆	☆	
Loss function analysis		☆	☆	☆
Mean time between failures	☆			☆
Plant capability index		☆		☆
Planning systems & expectations	☆	☆	☆	☆
Process mapping — 3D	☆	☆	☆	☆
Process re-engineering/dissection	☆	☆	☆	
Statistical process control		☆		☆
The 5 why's		☆	☆	
World class indicators	☆		☆	
Low level tools				
Pareto	☆	☆	☆	☆
Check sheet		☆		☆
Histograms		☆		☆
Scatter diagrams		☆		☆
Control chart		☆		☆

Figure 9.1   Quality tools available

HIGHER-LEVEL TOOLS

Added value analysis

Method

At the end of each process within a system, the output is valued in financial terms. This procedure effectively generates a sales value for each stage within the system.

The input resources consumed by the transformation process are then valued.

Value added represents the difference between the total valuation of inputs and lost resources, and the total value of the outputs. The values may include time, monetary value and opportunity cost value.

Results

The calculations highlight value reducing sections as well as low value adding sections. Some organizations extend the principles and impute values where no external comparison is possible.

Care must be taken when applying this technique because the

concept must be applied consistently to all the processes within an organization so that true comparison between alternative options is possible. The sum of the parts of added value must be no greater than the total added value created by the company.

Identifying the processes themselves can be exceptionally difficult in some instances because some processes reduce values so that later processes may add greater value. Expert assistance should be sought where necessary.

Cost benefit analysis

Method

The known costs of implementing each alternative action are valued financially.

For each alternative being considered, benefits are financially valued according to the policy guidelines of the organization. The policy will declare the value put on items such as loss of life (for government purposes approximately £500,000) and the loss of available working time (usually calculated at the national average annual pay rate).

The net balance of the figures for each option shows whether a net benefit or a net cost would result from the actions.

Results

Quality can be allocated specific values for certain situations and decisions can be made that will provide the maximum amount of benefit to users. The difficulty with this method is that the financial evaluation of a qualitative issue usually depends upon the standpoint of the observer. For example, the value of wasted time caused by traffic jams on the M25 may equate to, say, £5.00 per hour per person on average to the economy, but to the individual rushing for a meeting £50 per hour may be insufficient.

Planning systems and expectations

Although these are not normally recognized as quality tools, planning systems are the main methods through which the organization decides upon the acceptable levels of performance from which quality criteria are specified. Expectations expressed in the planning methods are central to measuring quality performance and will determine how any improvement is received by users.

Many different items could be used under this heading, including budgets, five-year plans, three-year plans, expectations analysis, economic forecasts, competitor analysis and international trade reviews.

Loss function analysis — Taguchi

Method

A performance target is designed for the process in terms that can be clearly measured. For example, telephones will be answered on the first ring. The loss function is the amount of difference between actual performance achieved, and target performance.

Results

The analysis of the causes of discrepancy from target is crucial to the eventual elimination of all variance. Small changes in key inputs to the process can be monitored and, because the results show which have the most dramatic effect, operators can zero in on those elements. For example, the telephone system can monitor those phones that are not answered immediately so that resources may be re-allocated to the departments requiring assistance.

Failure mode and effect analysis (FMEA)

Method

The product is dissected into all of its elements. Potential problems with each element and group of elements is classified, scored and prioritized against three criteria:

1. severity of failure;
2. probability of recurrence;
3. probability of non-recurrence.

Groups of causes of failure can be chosen and the resulting effects highlighted.

Results

Analysis of the risk and value of each kind of failure is used to determine priorities and to value and rank outcomes. This method can be used to apply 'Normal distribution' techniques to failures and their outcomes in order to minimize overall risk to the organization.

Fishbone, cause/effect, fault tree analysis

Method

Detailed analyses of events are produced to show how a process is composed of many events. The analysis is very similar to critical flow path analysis, except that the components are shown as if they are parts of a fish skeleton. Process flows are drawn in which each of the lines represents an event that supports or leads to another event.

These diagrams are usually kept simple to explain how visible effects were caused by previous operations and not by the sector in which the problem becomes obvious. Figure 9.2 illustrates a fishbone diagram.

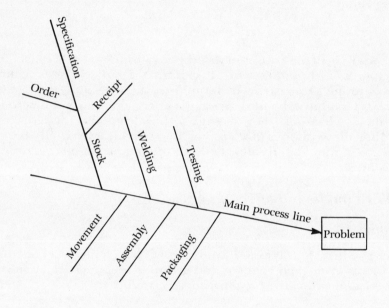

Figure 9.2   Fishbone diagrams

Results

Clear explanations of the causes of the difficulties enables everyone to understand and agree on the necessary corrective action.

This chart can be directly developed into critical path analysis by awarding values, probabilities or risk values to the events and relationships shown.

Process mapping — 3D

Method

This technique is also known as Physical Event Mapping or Event Mapping.

By interviewing a representative section of the employees of an organization, a generic map is drawn of the actual processes involved in providing customers with products or services. These maps show the practical short-cuts that staff operate and not the procedures expected by management.

Multi-levels may be used to demonstrate operational, tactical or strategic views of the organization. Multi-dimensions are used to show the impact and importance of different departments, work load, quality levels and other important criteria on throughput and related processes.

Results

This technique is used to re-engineer processes across an organization, remove duplication, reduce cost, restructure management, identify how to increase market penetration and to solve many other problems. The organization is able to understand how changes to fundamental processes can affect the whole organization by interpreting the dimensions. Manpower and resource implications can be estimated and modelled to define the most suitable implementation path. Incremental change can be introduced to minimize traumatic effects on staff who are crucial to the well-being of continued operations.

This technique relies on the competence of management and the willingness of staff to pursue their ideals in a practical manner.

An elementary example of this technique was shown in Figure 7.2.

Process re-engineering, process dissection

Method

All of the tasks performed within an operation are defined clearly by means of flow chart techniques. Initial analysis is usually performed at operational levels, within departments or sections, to ascertain that benefit is feasible. Details of processes are shown in flow diagrams or charts so that either specialists or staff can see how improvement may be made.

This technique can be developed from critical path analysis.

Results

By removing duplications and unnecessary processes in order to reduce costs, and by reducing the amount of time consumed in producing output, great improvements are made possible. Work can be eliminated to a large extent if the organization is fearless in applying the findings of a project.

The system relies on experts in information technology being available to design and implement systems to facilitate improvement.

Benchmarking

Method

Data on a department's or organization's performance can be compared with either internal or external data.

Important criteria relating to critical processes are defined by management, eg the number of man years required to assemble a car, the number of guests that a waiter/waitress is expected to serve, or the number of manual tasks completed per manufactured television tube.

Management information from competitors or organizations operating similar processes is exchanged to create a table showing key performance, quality and cost data. For example, a table comparing the numbers of finance function staff employed by motor vehicle manufacturers would show that UK and US companies employ significantly more personnel than their Japanese competitors.

Results

Critical differences between the organizations under review are highlighted in order to decide whether alternative methods or processes could be used to solve problems or improve performance against targets and objectives. The best practices within the group may be defined and shared so that each organization benefits from the knowledge.

Few organizations swap data specifically concerning their finance functions, but a few comparisons of the numbers employed are known to have been made. Ford Motor in the US, employing 400 people in accounts payable, was surprised to find that a similar sized Toyota plant only employed 15 people to perform the same functions.

Statistical process control (SPC)

Method

SPC is the method of controlling processes by analyzing sample results taken from those processes. This method is favoured by most quality experts as it introduces fundamental control disciplines into otherwise uncontrolled environments.

Samples are regularly taken from the output of a process, the sample size being defined by the volume throughput and frequency of sampling. Data is compiled and expressed as either normal curves or as points on a normal curve.

Results

The position of the results of the sampling determines whether the process is within overall control. The process is within control if the mean of the data remains constant at the point specified for the process.

The objective is to keep the process within control and not to become too concerned with the degree of failure. Normal failure is acceptable, because by definition there will be extra successful output.

The normal curve has a number of important characteristics:

☐ The top of the curve shows the most probable result of the measurement.
☐ Each side of the bell shape is symmetrical.
☐ Standard deviations describe the relative distance from the mean of a particular result.
☐ Results of samples can relate to the sample itself, and to other external (previous) results.

The basic mathematics are:

Mean = average of all of the results.

$$\text{Standard deviation} = \sqrt{\frac{\text{(Sum of all differences from mean}}{\text{(Number of observations} - 1)}}$$

The process is said to be in control as long as individual test results lie within 1.96 standard deviations from the mean. (Figure 9.3 illustrates the normal curve.)

When comparing the distribution curves of different samples from the same process, curves should be closely aligned with one another. If the curves are not aligned, the process is out of control. Mathematics can test for this eventuality.

The 5 Why's

Method

When a problem occurs, asking 'why' five times can lead the questioner to the root cause of the problem. For example:

1. Why was the telephone service supplier paid late?
2. Because the invoice was processed late. Why?
3. Because the invoice was returned to finance late. Why?
4. Because the engineer had not raised the order. Why?
5. Because orders for services are not raised.

Resolution: either orders for services must be raised, or the system requirement for orders should be modified to allow payment for services without orders being raised.

Results

Discussion and debate will be enhanced by staff addressing the causes of difficulty and not the symptoms. This technique stops individuals from thinking about the symptoms and forces them

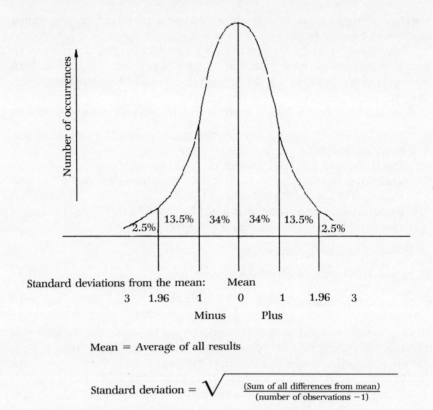

Figure 9.3 The normal curve

into considering the root causes of problems, from which solutions can be generated.

World class indicators

Method

These indicators are a development of the benchmarking technique and use data from many companies throughout the world in order to discover the world's best performance. Basic measures include such things as time taken to produce comparable units, failure rate, number of employees per unit, number of indirect staff per direct worker, etc. Individual company achievements are then rated as percentages of the world's best achievement against each criterion.

Results

The indicators have value in that they allow direct, non-financial comparison between international organizations. In this way, exchange rates, working practices and other irrelevant criteria are avoided in the comparison and a table of relative performance is created. For this reason, most vehicle manufacturers state their performance in terms of vehicles manufactured per man year.

Mean time between failures

Method

Data is collected about the different kinds of failure of a product used by consumers. The causes of failure are identified and grouped according to severity, impact, cost or other criteria. Representative failures within each group are selected to illustrate particular grades of failure.

Products are tested to enable failures to be scored and compared, based on the mean time between the failures identified.

Results

Customer/consumer satisfaction can be assessed on competing services. The base line customer expectation of quality can be defined for complex services so that performance can be gauged. The impact of small changes can be assessed to discover whether increasing or reducing tolerances would affect overall performance. Large samples are required for this kind of analysis.

This tool is difficult to apply within the finance function.

Plant capability index

Method

The manufacturing proficiencies required in order to produce a product are listed, in a similar way to the specification of product components. This normally shows the kind of process and, more importantly, the tolerances to which the product or service must be delivered.

The processing capabilities of the particular plant under scrutiny are scored against component design requirements. These statistical measures define the operating margins or 'band width' for the plant or machine in the categories listed.

When applying this technique within a finance function, individual competencies can be assessed so that work may be allocated to the most suitable and qualified person.

Results

When a customer seeks to decide which plants will be allowed to supply products, plant capability indices allow direct, non-financial comparison. This technique may be applied when comparing different service providers because staff and employees can be assessed in the same way as plant can be scored and evaluated.

Critical path analysis

Method

The flow of the processes and events within the system that creates the output of the organization is reproduced as a diagram. Important relationships are shown as lines between the boxes that represent particular events.

Probabilities and expected timings are associated with particular events.

The events that cumulatively take the longest period of time between the decision points represent the critical path.

Results

Those events that must be completed within certain time-scales are identified. Schedules can be constructed so that the risk from failing to complete any single process is minimized. To achieve goals within the specified time-frame, the project champion frequently uses the critical points as milestones to mark progress within the project.

LOW-LEVEL TOOLS

Pareto

This statistical technique is the mathematics which shows that 80 per cent of the result is generated from 20 per cent of the causes. It is more commonly known as the 80/20 rule.

All of the factors that affect a known measure are listed in order of importance. Pareto suggests that one-fifth of the factors will account for four-fifths of the evaluated response from all of those factors.

By using this technique, organizations can separate the essential actions from the ineffective.

Figure 9.4 shows the Pareto effect.

Check sheets

These are pre-printed pieces of paper used to collect information in predefined ways, for example pre-printed order forms requiring only ticks to order items.

Histograms

Histograms are graphs that use vertical bars to illustrate the relative size of one factor against another.

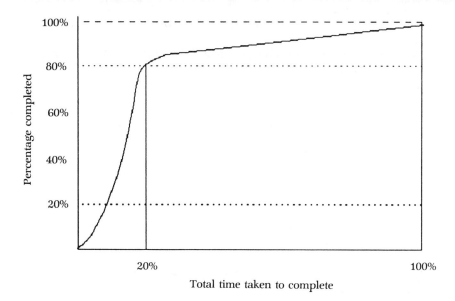

The axes are frequently used to describe:

stock costs compared to numbers of units involved
numbers of problems to number of causes
value of improvements to number of actions possible
speed of learning to number of iterations of task

Figure 9.4   The Pareto effect

Scatter diagrams

These are diagrams or graphs which pin-point with dots the many results from tests. They show clusters and groups that would otherwise remain undetected. Because there are no lines joining the points on the chart, the diagram is called a scatter diagram.

These charts are most useful in showing that relationships exist where statistical mathematics is unable to find any relationship.

Control charts

Graph paper is used to predefine the ranges within which the results of a test are acceptable. Usually this involves calculating the limits of 95 per cent probability that a sample is acceptable and showing the values as upper and lower limits on a chart.

When output samples are tested, all results are checked

against the chart. If the results are outside acceptance limits, either the whole output should be tested or the batch should be failed.

Control charts can also be used by staff to decide whether action should or should not be taken.

10

Checking Implementation

This chapter includes a series of checklists designed to help readers remember important topics relating to particular subjects.

THE IMPLEMENTATION OF QUALITY

The objective of the process of implementation is practical achievement. During implementation two measures are crucial:

- ☐ the extent of any improvement;
- ☐ the speed of the achievement.

To encourage and aid successful accomplishment, those points at which success has been achieved must be recognized and highlighted. For this reason implementation has to be planned so that monitoring and publication and assessment of results between interested parties can be meaningful.

The primary stages within implementation are:

Pre-project planning:	Why, where, who, how and when, management.
Develop common understanding:	Management, staff, groups and committees, language.
Start the ball rolling:	Management, resources, identifying solutions, taking action.
Build momentum:	Succession, responsibility, authority.

Throughout each of these stages, an environment has to be constructed and nurtured in which success is recognized and rewarded and failure is corrected or, preferably, avoided. The main routes to successful quality project management are:

Patience:	Do not expect leaps of imagination or performance.
Logical:	Incremental improvements must follow in a reasoned and understandable sequence.
Ascending:	Always seek to improve, but allow flexibility for initiatives to appear to move sideways and then upwards. Occasionally, backward steps may be necessary to achieve a higher ultimate objective.
Realistic:	Take account of individual competencies, abilities and personal needs. Build in flexibility of response so that different levels of awareness of quality do not cause conflict.
Communicate:	Distribute information to those that need data and to those that may be interested. Increase the internal and external recognition of achievement.
Generate 'want':	By applying quality disciplines to the whole organization and its methods, develop in individuals the need to reach ever-higher goals. Make the quality initiative a personal issue.

PRE-PROJECT PLANNING

The potential success of a project is frequently determined even before the initiative has been accepted for implementation. As early discussions take place, the size of the project, the subject and the likely scale of benefit will be decided. Because these early decisions limit and constrain the potential success of the project during implementation, great attention should be paid to them. The decision to pursue the quality initiative within the finance function or within the organization as a whole should be taken after ensuring that the pre-requisites are met. These essential ingredients will depend upon individual circumstances, but the greatest undeniable need is the commitment of top management.

Unless the organization has this commitment, a quality programme will certainly result in partial failure. Most failures can be avoided by embarking on an early training programme for top management in order to convince them of the benefits.

When the understanding and commitment is in place, questions concerning the scope and scale of the project can be decided. Each project has to have a leader who commands authority within the organization and who can communicate the vision of the future. A sponsor for the project should be found who matches business needs with personal characteristics. Sponsorship implies both a commitment to the objectives and an ability to assign resources to the project. The stature, credibility and authority of the sponsor plays a critical role in determining the success of projects and whether an initiative is pursued throughout the company. Supporting the leader and the sponsor is the champion, who is able to take action and to drive and motivate colleagues to initiate and then implement change.

The result of the pre-project planning is a defined strategy that can be communicated to employees in terms of:

- ☐ named individuals to lead, sponsor and drive the initiative;
- ☐ reasons for change;
- ☐ objectives;
- ☐ targets for achievement;
- ☐ methods for making implementation practical.

1: SETTING UP A PROJECT

Management   Commitment is essential

Why   Identify and show the reasons for the initiative. Preliminary definition of the benefits

Where   Early suggestions for targets and priorities

Who   Recommendations for allocating responsibility and identification of the sponsor and champion. Set up an implementation team

How   Define what must be understood by staff — the causes and the route forward
Outline of methodology to be adopted — including estimated requirements for implementation personnel, special training, and financial and non-financial resources.

When   Provisional setting of deadlines, including necessary allocations for the implementation team and other members of staff

2: SETTING OBJECTIVES

- ☐ Understand the business
- ☐ Discover and understand the customers' and users' needs
- ☐ Satisfy those needs
- ☐ Improve service performance constantly
- ☐ Empower staff to act

3: DECIDING A STRATEGY

☐ Financial vision   ☐ Me too
☐ Piggy-back   ☐ Topic based

4: PRIORITIZING TARGETS

☐ Easiest   ☐ Largest payback
☐ Quickest   ☐ Least risk of failure

5: DEFINE THE TARGET

☐ Recognize the current level of quality
☐ Describe the level of quality sought
☐ Plan conversion to the desired level of quality
☐ Act today, don't leave it until tomorrow
☐ Maintain the impetus

TAKING THE FIRST STEPS — THE KINGS FUND

Background

The Fund became an independent charity by Act of parliament in 1907. Over the years its main tasks have developed into fulfilling four main functions: grant-making — helping London Health Services; information centre — supporting innovations in the NHS; college — raising management standards in the NHS; institute — improving the quality of public debate about health policy.

Point of view: Financial Director

Apart from supporting the primary functions of the Fund, the main objective of the finance function is to help management, staff and officers understand much more of the wider perspective of the work of the fund. By doing so, the Fund may lose some of the shroud of mystery but it will gain from better achievement of its objectives.

The devolvement and information improvement initiatives are currently driven more by computer systems than by management. There is always something better to spend money on than computers.

The management board understands that just having numbers available on which to base decisions is not sufficient. We are developing better systems to report on work content and milestones as well as the financial aspects.

Key data and performance indicators will provide a much better core of information on which to base our decisions.

The starting point has to be getting information right at the point of initiation — the person ordering the supplies.

Budgetary information is totally financial at the moment. Though this is inadequate for our real needs, we have to start forecasting somewhere.

The basic actual data that we have is improving in quality as those who have responsibility receive the data for which they are accountable. The process of educating all staff to understand that an account code is the means by which income and expenditure statements are produced is a long one.

Financial people must not work in isolation but with those to whom the decision-making authority has been delegated.

Guidelines

1   Make sure that the people who do things decide the changes to be made.
2   Do not design for professionals — design for the customers.
3   Give the tools to those who need them, not head office.
4   Use specialist skills where they are needed.
5   Keep support staff numbers to as few as possible.
6   Encourage more and more open communications.

Comment

Finance is a facilitator to service, not a constraint. It should make life easier. The department has been too used to saying 'No', probably because so few others have understood the financial numbers involved.

DEVELOP A COMMON PLATFORM OF UNDERSTANDING

Within the organization each individual and group has their own particular set of attitudes and beliefs. Complete agreement between all of these disparate parties may never be feasible but a satisfactory compromise is possible. For finance function personnel, the development of the ability to compromise and reach agreement is essential before deciding what action to take. Moreover, a common understanding of the problems and alternative solutions is necessary for three reasons:

1.   Finance personnel are often the key to communication within the whole organization, as they have access to, and influence with, other functions.
2.   Finance usually drives the administration and all the non-productive functions of the company. Correct identification of the root causes of problems is crucial.
3.   In many organizations finance is gradually progressing from being back-room oriented to front-room and customer driven. This requires a team approach to problem solving, not personal solutions.

When employees have gained an awareness of their environment and the likely impact of their decisions, they will be able to understand each other's position. On the basis of new understanding and awareness, compromise can be achieved. Achieving this understanding can come from addressing the attitudes of:

☐ management;
☐ individual employees;
☐ groups or committees.

By using a tripartite approach, ingrained difficulties such as the 'us and them' attitude and lack of team working will be overcome. Failing to gain a common understanding among individual staff invariably leads to misunderstanding and conflict. The result of intra-organizational management misunderstanding is conflict and the pursuit of opposing goals. When groups or committees are involved in conflict, neither party is likely to achieve its objectives, and so the whole organization suffers.

To take an example of this, a manufacturing subsidiary of an international company based its production schedule on the demand forecast from the sales subsidiary in 1991. When the expected sales in 1992 did not materialize, manufacturing made for stock; sales failed to notify forecast changes. When finished goods stock rose to 180 days, group management were forced to take decisive action to reduce stocks by discounted selling.

The cause of the problem revolved around production staff being assessed by how much was produced, and sales staff by how much was sold.

If quality principles had been applied to the budgeting process, the resulting financial losses would not have arisen in the first place.

6: DEVELOP UNDERSTANDING

Management

☐ At least a minimum level of commitment must be present before a project may start. Educate, persuade and cajole until the commitment exists
☐ Teach managers how to work as a team, generating cross-disciplinary trust
☐ Teach how to delegate without losing control
☐ Test employee competence so that gaps in knowledge or weaknesses can be filled early in the programme
☐ Create an understanding of how to recognize Quality
☐ Assess the current level of quality. Illustrate the benefits of improving to a different level
☐ Complete a SWOT analysis for the function within the organization in order to identify its critical success factors

Individual employees

☐ Teach all staff how to use the quality tools
☐ Teach listening and learning abilities
☐ Help employees to recognize their own personal attitudes and to make comparison with their peer group
☐ Identify individuals' position in the improvement channel — define targets for learning, training and empowerment
☐ Recognize and develop strengths
☐ Demonstrate the differences between spoken beliefs and true beliefs
☐ Facilitate employee understanding of their role in their function, section and whole organization
☐ Develop champions for initiatives
☐ Set up awards and prizes and publish information regularly
☐ Increase personal satisfaction through communication and recognition

Groups and committees of multi-function staff

☐ Teach groups how to work together
☐ Use simulation and training to teach and improve working methods
☐ Demonstrate how to solve practical problems
☐ Encourage better listening abilities
☐ Teach meeting management
☐ Use group techniques to gain mutual recognition and resolve common problems
☐ Demonstrate how conflict can be minimized and managed positively

7: THE WORK CYCLE

☐ Feedback
☐ Support
☐ Learn
☐ Inform
☐ Experience
☐ Conceptualize
☐ Test
☐ Accept
☐ Select
☐ Develop strategy

☐ Short list
☐ Plan to introduce
☐ Educate providers
☐ Announce
☐ Educate users
☐ Build infrastructure
☐ Timing
☐ Location
☐ Construct
☐ Deliver

8: FEEDBACK CHANNELS

☐ In person
☐ Through representatives

☐ Committees
☐ Surrogates

☐ Through advisers   ☐ Questionnaires
☐ Multi-user groups

9: THE EMPLOYMENT CYCLE

Pre-employment   Identify need
                        Screening
                        Choose

Employ   Induction
                        Priority setting
                        Behaviour conditioning
                        Define expectations

Deploy   Set objectives
                        Communicate
                        Feedback

Develop   Identify potential
                        Succession planning

Retire   Exit checks

10: CONSIDERING PEOPLE

☐ Leader with vision   ☐ Provide useful experience
☐ Sponsor with authority   ☐ Empower where possible
☐ Champion with commitment   ☐ Adopt suitable leadership style
☐ Educate generally   ☐ Use outside help where necess-
☐ Train specifically   ary

11: PROVIDING THE SERVICE

☐ Positive attitude   ☐ Seek out improvements
☐ Flexible response   ☐ Look for 'mould-breaking' improve-
☐ Listen and think   ments
☐ Discuss — do not tell   ☐ Plan
☐ Help users   ☐ Work to the plan
☐ Teach users and colleagues   ☐ Do not change the plan
☐ Learn from others

12: WORK CONTENT

Data   Accurate, consistent, complete
Presentation Timely, relevant, useful, understandable

Environment   Dates, scale, scope, planning, influencing factors
Alternatives, opportunities, threats
Implications, parallel initiatives, balance of emphasis
Risk analysis, trends, problems
Assumptions

Action   Approriateness, timeliness

MAINTAINING THE MOMENTUM FOR CHANGE — RTM MANAGEMENT CONSULTANTS

Background

The company specializes in helping companies that wish to achieve certain quality standards. Most client companies want to gain BS 5750 certification, though some are looking to adopt a TQM approach. Consultancy periods last between two months and two years, depending on needs. The client base tends to be small/medium-sized organizations employing up to 500 staff.

Point of view: Robin Tidd MBA FCMA — Managing Director

Most of our clients want to improve their operations in the minimum amount of time possible. Quality is the route for almost every company, like it or not.

Managing directors generally understand what quality is and some are beginning to realize what quality is not. Superficial answers and quick-fix solutions are not in the vocabulary of a real quality company.

The culture of companies usually has to change; the whole philosophy has to evolve so that employees are trusted and personal contribution is recognized. This is not easy for 'old school' managers to accept, but when they do it works marvellously. Flesh and blood considerations are critical to a business, more important than any other single factor.

Quality cannot fail if it is implemented correctly. Many people make the mistake of applying formulas without thinking (especially where external consultants are used) and such initiatives frequently fail.

The enemies of quality are many, though the main ones are readily avoidable. They are:

☐ Short termism.
☐ Where quality is not company-wide but applies to only one department, creating victims.
☐ Attributing problems to people, as opposed to attributing solutions to systems.
☐ The lack of a system to continually improve the business. An important key to successful implementation is the ability of staff to see and understand the role of all the other departments and personnel.

We resolve the problem of staff not seeing how their own work causes problems for others, by using the 'blind spot matrix'. This chart helps show where the root cause of difficulties lies, and how the difficulties can be resolved.

Blind Spot Matrix

Problems: Prevented in:	Visible in department: A	B	C	D	Customer complaint	Total problems
A	1,2,3	4,5,6	7,8,9,10	11,12,13	14,15	15
B		16,17,18	19,20,21	22,23	24,25	10
C			26,27,28	29	30	5
D				31,32,33	34	4
Total	3	6	10	9	6	34

Note: Problems 4 to 6 are solved in B, caused by A. Blind spots are shaded areas.

Normally management and staff can see the problems that they have caused in their own department. In the above example, 12 problems would be visible of a possible 34. All other cross-references are blind spots where faulty actions impact on others and are permanently tolerated. There is no improvement strategy for 22 of 34 of the problems in the above example. Blind spots often account for more than 80 per cent of problems. Departments eradicate known problems but do not see the effect of their actions downstream.

In the hands of skilled users, this matrix is an influential tool for identifying problem-solving actions. The 'not our fault' syndrome is exposed in the glare of peer group pressure and put right. The objective is to monitor problems and quantify them. Errors are opportunities for making improvement. The culture must encourage the exposure of problems and the finding of resolutions.

The finance function plays a key role in most organizations and must be led by forward-thinking management. All too often finance has been left out of initiatives, resulting in a poorer level of decision-making than would otherwise be possible. Important issues concerning financial information must be addressed, such as:

1. Whether standard and process costing systems can have a role when products are customer specific — average costing produces average results.
2. Where job costing is used to evaluate the efficiencies of jobs, would the time be better spent studying the processes that produce those Jobs?
3. What is the benefit of comparison with some arbitrary budget when the object is not to 'do as well as we said we would', but to 'do as well as we can', without limit?
4. Budgets can constrain performance improvement if strongly managed.

A great deal of financial reporting is what we term discretionary work, in that it is produced in the knowledge that it adds no value directly. It may be of use to the spectators of the business (shareholders, banks, etc) but it is not used for managing the business. Volumes of data are also produced for managers — historical records of job profits, inter-departmental allocations, profit centre profit and loss statements — many of which are positively misleading. Many of these reports are 'damage reports' and status indicators to managers. There are better and cheaper ways of producing information which is more informative for managers.

Guidelines

1. Do not try to gain a quality finance function alone — it is a part of the overall business.
2. Get the quality passion throughout the organization.
3. Teach the quality science to all employees — understand the philosophy.
4. Enlist real leadership to provide the vision for the business or service.
5. Use specialists to help the top team in particular, and other staff if required.

Useful tips

1. Do not use middle management for patching up lower-level problems.
2. Accountants should be cross-functional teachers of the whole quality ethos.
3. Take great care when using accountants to teach others, as they often believe that they stand in judgement of the rest of the organization. Encourage them to become team players and cast off their role as judge.
4. Do not change processes until you have an identified state of stability. Change where there is no stability will give unsatisfactory results.
5. Address the cultural problems first, to remove any fear of exposure of faults. Fear can control the environment and can therefore control data.

START THE BALL ROLLING

With a strategy in place and employees understanding both the vision and the route towards that vision, practical change then has to be encouraged.

Early in quality initiatives staff will test whether management really mean what they say by doing something unexpected or unusual. The response will be closely monitored by the employees to determine whether quality is another method of extracting more unrewarded labour or a genuine opportunity for everyone to improve their lot. If management show negative attitudes or fail to back up change, the whole project may falter and achieve much less than was intended. Positive reward or recognition for the first stages of change will provide essential support and encouragement to others. As staff become more accustomed to making minor change, bigger tasks will be approached and improvement will gather momentum.

13: GETTING STARTED

General finance functions

☐ Dissect the work content and create a process map
☐ Identify genuine requirements
☐ First make sure that work is effective
☐ Match skills to work requirement
☐ Plan the normal work load
☐ Plan for abnormal work loads
☐ Plan to make changes, include flexible response
☐ When a plan is agreed, keep to it
☐ Simplify the processes
☐ Minimize cycles times
☐ Standardize, with flexibility
☐ Use common terminology
☐ Prioritize work
☐ Educate customers
☐ Evaluate staff for training needs
☐ Set up training and learning schools
☐ Encourage feedback and act on requests
☐ Set up relevant measures
☐ Measure at the perimeters
☐ Always measure
☐ Use external figures to compare with own results — benchmark
☐ Always complete post-project analysis
☐ Benefit from hindsight

Specific to financial information providers

☐ Automate processes where possible and sensible
☐ Recognize bottleneck people
☐ Teach the users to understand more
☐ Set up information request specifications — as long as they do not slow the system
☐ Recognize different skills and different needs, and match them
☐ Establish simple bases of data — chart of accounts
☐ Ensure singular processing, ie once only, no duplications
☐ Show and justify assumptions
☐ Define simple presentation formats, clarify terms
☐ Limit complexity to match the needs
☐ Recognize risk
☐ Clarify the implications

Specific to financial service providers

☐ Plan for normal throughput
☐ Manage the work flow to reduce peaks and troughs

- ☐ Manage the work flow, before adjusting capacity
- ☐ Recognize the bottleneck services
- ☐ Plan work to maximize utilisation of bottleneck people
- ☐ Match skills and competence to demands
- ☐ Improve staff through training and education
- ☐ Educate the users and customers
- ☐ Set up feedback loops
- ☐ Use standard terminology
- ☐ Plan to make improvements
- ☐ Set realistic targets
- ☐ Define time-scales for improvement
- ☐ Monitor through statistical process control (SPC) where appropriate

14: MEASUREMENT

Categories	Prevention
	Appraisal
	Failure
Divisions	Actual costs
	Opportunity costs
Levels	Strategic, tactical, operational
Easiest	At perimeter or boundary
	Against quality acceptance criteria

- ☐ Analyze trends.

15: BREAKING DOWN TIME

Total	From the employee
System	Identified as used by the employee
Wasted	Not identified as used by the employee
Cycle	Total required to produce services
Processing	Identified as consumed by service provision
Lost	Time when service was not being worked on

STEP BY STEP — BRITISH AEROSPACE, SYSTEMS AND SERVICES DIVISION

Background

The division was formed in September 1991 to focus attention more closely on customer and business needs. The business is involved in the provision of fully integrated defence services and systems to very high standards of security, accuracy and performance.

The business revolves around the management and control of very complex projects based on a number of contracts which provide the goods and services required by the customers.

Point of View: Head of management accounting

The finance function keeps our managers both financially aware and 'in line'. Our aim it to provide good business advice. Management accounting sees all of the issues because it is the business that matters to us, rather than just the numbers. Because we cross all departmental boundaries, we have a breadth of vision not available to most other sections.

Our main function is to help manage the conflicting objectives of minimum cost with the need to deliver a fully developed work package and associated support to our customers. This is a very difficult line to tread and is especially complex in a defence environment. Assumptions, underlying data and other facts are verified by us before information is published; the basic data we publish has to be accurate and very timely. Late information is frequently worse than useless; we now insist on timeliness.

The division has taken numerous quality initiatives since its formation and we have obtained part 2 certification for ISO 9001. Although the objective is most laudable, the process of proceduralization is not fully convincing.

Our progress has been quite structured in approach and was built from the following:

☐ Establish the mission.
☐ Recognize the critical success factors.
☐ Complete the SWOT analysis.
☐ Analyze the needs.
☐ Choose the methods and systems.

Before some of the recent initiatives, we found that process improvement initiatives failed because they did not address the 'people issues'. Forms were redesigned but the culture within the divisions remained unchanged. Quality has to change the way that people relate to one another. The goal has to be common, visible and available to all.

The quality initiative has been an interesting experience, and the division has benefited enormously. The long-term benefits will be substantial, but the cost is also significant.

As with any important project, the quality manager has to be the driver, if not the champion, of the initiative — and that person must be chosen with great care. He or she must be the champion of attitudes, not procedures.

Guidelines

1. The overall sponsor must be the person at the top.
2. Management re-education from the top down is required.
3. Maintain a single-minded approach.
4. Make change a habit, ensure cross-functional communication.
5. Work to very tight deadlines.
6. Create personal responsibility — insist the chairman phone the managers.

7. Use feedback to improve, and always improve.
8. Get staff to think about what they do.
9. Ensure added value is generated by you personally and by all your staff.
10. Insist on 'right first time' from all your staff and suppliers.
11. Re-vitalise the process, stop the organization going back to its old ways.

APPLYING QUALITY TOOLS TO FINANCE

The practical application of quality tools can reveal surprising statistics which make staff think about the context and results of their work. Examples of applying the tools are shown below and potential results are highlighted within the finance function context.

Using process mapping in finance

There are two ways of mapping processes:

1. Within the section, showing all the tasks performed on a flow chart.

    If staff work together to prepare this type of analysis, they will begin to recognize how much time is wasted and be able to reduce work substantially.

    A quick way of working this method is to use 'Post-it' notes with the name of the task stuck on to a white board to show the flow of work.

2. For the organization, map out all the processes crucial to the customer and consumer. Overlay a sheet of acetate, on to which are drawn the tasks performed within finance, positioned over the events that add value for the customer.

    Where the department performs tasks that are unimportant to the customer, consider the effect of not doing that task. Where the task is important to the customer, giving added value, consider new ways of reducing the time taken to set up, perform and clean up.

These techniques are also very useful in assessing the effectiveness of information systems, and where new systems and methods could benefit from investment.

Pareto in the finance function

The Pareto principle is far from being absolutely accurate but it can be interpreted to identify problems and generate prioritized solutions. This simplistic form of statistical control is expressed by the 80/20 rule in which 80 per cent of the output is usually explained by 20 per cent of the input. By targeting emphasis and encouragement, the tool may be used to decide and weight responses, and to redress balances within the organization.

The method involves taking measurements of the process identified for improvement and grouping results under the various headings discovered as being the causes of errors or problems. The sum of the results should be displayed in order of size, a histogram charted of the individual amounts and a cumulative chart drawn showing the individual amounts. Figure 10.1 shows an example of Pareto usage.

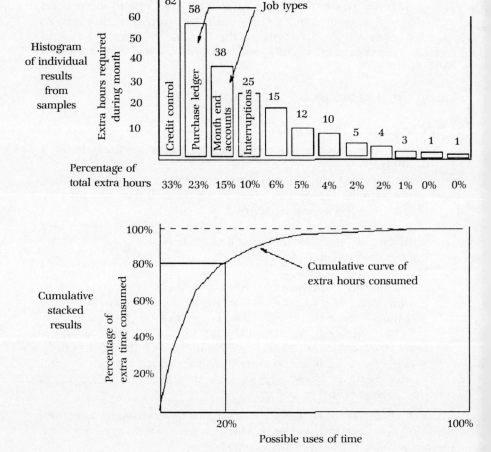

Figure 10.1 Example of Pareto useage

Using statistical process control in finance

This technique may be applied to any situation in which a task is repeated and measurable consistency is required. The methodology is based on the fact that when samples are taken of consistent and repetitive output, the distribution of the deviation in results is said to be normal. Normal distribution should exist in the results of a flowing system of production that is in equilibrium. If the system is subject to change caused by external forces, the normal curve may be skewed or affected in some way.

In outline, the principles are as follows:

- ☐ Identify the process to be measured and specify sampling tests to ensure that clear and consistent results should be obtained.
- ☐ Allow tests to be taken at random, with great frequency.
- ☐ Decide how many samples must be taken to provide a valid result and define the frequency of the testing.
- ☐ Plot the results of each sample on a chart prepared to monitor the process.
- ☐ Using statistical techniques, or a control chart, decide whether the process is within control.
- ☐ If the process is not within control, take action to correct the performance of the sequence of events.

The results of applying quality tools

Examples of the application of the Pareto technique are as follows:

1. Removing processes
Twenty per cent of processes perform or control 80 per cent of the output requirements in purchase or sales ledgers.

By concentrating on 20 per cent of processes to be standardized and formalized, many others may be discontinued or amalgamated.

2. Standardizing documents
Eighty per cent of the input needs of a single system can be gathered from one or two documents.

Using many similar documents for different processes is a potential source of error and misunderstanding for users. The data needs of most systems can be reduced dramatically. For example, goods received notes could act as sales returns tickets and be used to validate credit notes.

3. Reporting
Eighty per cent of the standard reports issued at the month end are unnecessary.

Asking users whether they actually use reports reveals who the real users are and which reports are unnecessary. Where this questioning is undertaken for the first time for many months, users usually ask for different and better information that fits their needs more closely. The process should be carefully controlled.

4. Cash

Eighty per cent of cash flow is generated by 20 per cent of the customers and invoices.

Developing good personal relations with customers will create an understanding of mutual needs and associated pressures.

Eighty per cent of supplier payments could be made automatically by self-bill, based on verified goods received, thus avoiding 80 per cent of the purchase ledger work normally associated with payments.

The Pareto technique is the quickest to identify action that should be taken to achieve positive results. The other tools can produce more significant results, though they may take a little longer to implement. Examples include:

1. Credit notes

As customer credit is issued the causes must be noted. Later analysis of the causes may result in action being taken, such as labelling improvements (in retail), format improvements to work done certificates (in construction), or increased staff training in the preparation of quotations (in manufacturing).

The dates on which invoices are paid by customers can be analyzed to show the normal number of days credit taken. The terms and conditions of trade should be reviewed for customers who extend their credit beyond two standard deviations from the mean. In this way, client specific prices can be produced and routine systems improved to highlight problem customers.

For those organizations that positively seek to issue more credits to customers in order to generate more business, statistical analysis can be used to improve the effectiveness of the marketing initiative (eg Little Chef restaurants giving discounts on weekend meals for weekday travellers).

2. Supplier payments

An organization should pay only for those goods and services that it has received. Processing orders, goods received notes and invoices represents three separate phases of work for most organizations. To avoid processing any purchase invoices, the goods received note can be treated as an invoice. Payment may then be made (subject to HM Customs & Excise rules) on the due date agreed. Some organizations have taken this to further stages, where:

☐ the order becomes both the goods inwards note and the invoice; or

☐ based on point of sale information, the manufacturer decides how much product to deliver to the retailer and raises a self-billed order, but no invoice. Payment is made up the supply chain based on the value of retail sales only.

If either of these approaches is adopted, the main benefits are that fewer staff will be employed (usually at least 75 per cent reduction in the purchase ledger section), and that there will be a dramatic simplification of overall business systems. The sharing of information, especially profitability and price sensitive data, is crucial to the success of such fundamental changes.

Many companies operate on the understanding that they will pay suppliers once they have a correct and authorized invoice. In fact, payment to the supplier can only be delayed (not avoided) by making various complex stipulations. Creating barriers to making payment will result in higher costs and unnecessary antagonism. Companies are mistaken if they believe that these methods and sharp practices improve either efficiency or effectiveness, or lower total costs. By penalizing the supplier the organization is ensuring that suppliers will pass on price increases sooner than they otherwise might.

3. Account coding errors

Coding errors can be eliminated if the input processing of all items is known by the user to be accurate. Inaccurate coding can be avoided by making the user responsible for the input. This strategy may require improved charts of accounts which use 'English' to facilitate simple and intelligent recognition by the user. Report generation in standard English could then allow users to fulfil their precise needs.

By applying Pareto, the journal entries that are used to correct accounts could be monitored by cause. Identification of fundamental problems will help to prioritize any extra training or system improvements needed.

4. Reporting

The organization may wish to reduce the days taken to produce monthly reports in order to increase the number of man days allowed to advise and assist with report definitions and interpretation.

By analyzing over a number of months any item of work occupying more than one hour, trends can be recognized and the causes of problems and the unnecessary consumption of time can be identified and avoided. This may result in the complete automation of duties such as prepayments and accruals. The principle of limiting the time allowed in which to perform functions can be extended to items such as:

☐ the number of man days taken to produce year end accounts;
☐ quarterly reviews for tax purposes;
☐ reconciliations and analyses of loans and leases outstanding;
☐ weekly updates of share register/options/contingencies;
☐ number of journals processed after the year end close.

16: QUALITY TOOLS

- ☐ Added value analysis
- ☐ Benchmarking
- ☐ Cost benefit analysis
- ☐ Critical path analysis
- ☐ Failure mode and effect analysis
- ☐ Fishbone, cause/effect, fault tree
- ☐ Loss function analysis
- ☐ Mean time between failures
- ☐ Plant capability index
- ☐ Planning systems and expectations

- ☐ Process mapping — 3D
- ☐ Process re-engineering/dissection
- ☐ Statistical process control
- ☐ The 5 why's
- ☐ World class indicators
- ☐ Pareto
- ☐ Check sheet
- ☐ Histograms
- ☐ Scatter diagrams
- ☐ Control chart

MAINTAINING THE DRIVE — LARGE UK MOTOR COMPANY

Background

This American-owned company is one of the largest vehicle manufacturing companies in the world. Their Essex-based UK operations are an important part of their European manufacturing. For over ten years they have been pursuing quality in their products and attitudes.

1991 and 1992 were exceptionally difficult years for the company and the organization declared substantial losses for both years. This financial pressure has increased both the requirement for change and the speed at which it must be implemented.

Quality is central to the company's approach to customers, suppliers and staff.

Point of view: Manager inward quality

Company policy over recent years has been changing dramatically in relation to our suppliers. Demand for our products is directly reflected in the levels of demand for the products of our suppliers — from this joint responsibility there has to be some kind of partnership.

In the old days, there was a simple formula to explain pricing:

Cost + profit = selling price.

This cosy relationship probably only existed in monopoly, or under supplied markets, and has not operated in the motor market for many years. Participants must realize that the market determines the selling price. Suppliers determine the external costs, and subsequently most of the internal costs.

Financial information affects whether certain decisions are made, the speed of implementation and the priorities. Timetables are frequently set as a result of financial input. However, the assessment of how improvements can be made starts with customers, and what they want and need.

We discuss jointly with suppliers how intended improvements can be made. Any financial benefits are shared between the customer, ourselves and the supplier.

We benchmark ourselves against our competition both financially and operationally. Our managers understand how important these comparisons are. Suppliers occasionally need more assistance to see the benefits of quality, so our training programmes, and special efficiency and effectiveness drives, play an important role in the relationship.

Until we set up the supplier development teams (SDTs), improvement was slow. Win/win situations are the objective and remarkable success has been achieved so far.

Quality is often misunderstood. Quality is never a cost. Cost will only be incurred if the organization did not know enough about its business in the first place.

Customer perceived quality can be expressed as a formula:

Quality = (perceived value) + (degree of delight) − (annoyance factor)
Perceived value is: Functionality divided by the cost of product
Degree of delight is: The extent to which the product exceeds expectations
Annoyance factor is: The importance of problems multiplied by the rate of recurrence

Over time, customer perceptions of the product will change. Unless the organization continually finds ways of providing more and better services and products for the customer, it will ultimately fail.

If you get the continual improvement right, you will stay ahead of the competition.

Guidelines

1. Understand the business objectives.
2. Understand the customer — using a tiering structure may help.
3. Interpret customer wants and desires closely — hold clinics if necessary.
4. Use graphical representation, not numbers, wherever possible.
5. Understand the whole life cycle.
6. Be utterly persistent.
7. Monitor anything that is important.

Comment

The concept of 'net material economics' may be of interest. This is where suppliers and manufacturers agree that an addition to a product or service is required but no revenue will be gained (eg the fitting of airbags in new cars). All of the parties concerned therefore work to minimize the total cost of the item — from design, materials and manufacture, to fitting and after sales service. This kind of thinking can only benefit the market overall.

GETTING HELP

Many individuals incorrectly believe that quality is an intuitive concept which can be assumed with ease. In almost every untrained case, the ingrained responses of western managers and staff mean that they are unable to recognize failures of quality until they understand quality concepts. For this reason, quality initiatives require specialist expertise. Recognizing that help is required is therefore an important step forward. Lack of experience in undertaking and managing quality initiatives usually leads organizations to consider using external consultants to assist with implementation programmes. The extent of the total resources required by the organization will depend upon the speed and depth of the programme envisaged.

External resources can be used to:

1. provide specialist facilitating assistance to the programme;
2. relieve work loads on staff to release them for new tasks;
3. take on new tasks to be handed over at a later date.

The extent to which external resources are used will depend on the organization's perceived needs in each of these areas, the availability of in-house resources and the speed of implementation necessary. Implementation alternatives are shown in Figure 10.2.

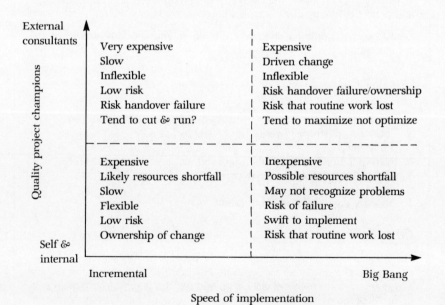

Figure 10.2 Implementation alternatives

Two sources of external expertise are commonly available:

☐ consultants;
☐ interim managers.

Consultants are sometimes more motivated by recognition from within their own company structure, whereas interim managers are likely to be motivated by success within the client company. Interim managers tend to work on their own account as sole traders, whereas consultants are often employed by companies or partnerships. Interim managers are priced at between £200 and £600 per day, while consultants charge fees that are in proportion to the anticipated benefits in the first year of operating the changes. These may work out at between £300 and £1,500. Interim managers are rather more difficult to find than consultants.

Employing external personnel can greatly assist hard-pressed senior staff to achieve more of their objectives, and more quickly. Applied sensibly, external help is both cost-effective and essential in providing skills that are not available internally. Consultants have to be managed as tightly as the quality project itself. They must work to defined targets and be measured and assessed during the course of the exercise.

17: GOLDEN RULES FOR USING CONSULTANTS

☐ State the objectives of the initiative
☐ Define the project clearly
☐ Define the benefits that the specialist must provide
☐ Clarify the start and finish dates, and any milestone dates
☐ Use a contract or formal agreement to document requirements
☐ Monitor progress frequently
☐ Define how extra work must be authorized before being started
☐ Be sure of consultant competence
☐ Make sure the consultant's face fits

KEEPING UP THE ENTHUSIASM — THIRD WAVE NHS TRUST HOSPITAL

Background

The Authority became one of the 'third wave' NHS Trusts in April 1993. It employs over 2,500 people on three major sites. Income of approximately £90m is generated by providing health care to almost 500,000 local inhabitants.

On becoming a trust, the post of director of information was created and a new director of finance was appointed. There are three finance managers — medicine, surgery and women and children's services.

Point of view: Finance manager — medicine

In 1992, quality became an important initiative that went right across the organization. Finance took an important part in a number of quality circle meetings that were held to put forward and discuss ideas for improvement. A number of changes were initiated, though the actual success of the teams was often dependent upon the individual who chaired the meeting — so some initiatives were less successful than we hoped.

Numerous solutions to problems required modifications to the computer information systems, though because the systems were rather old and scheduled for replacement, changes were never made.

At that time the authority applied for trust status within the NHS, and the massive organizational change that ensued caused the momentum to be lost. Since then, there has been a great deal of change in the organization and many of the issues are now being re-addressed. Three new directors have been appointed, including a director of quality, which should help a lot.

Guidelines

1. Do not attempt major organizational change and quality simultaneously.
2. Ensure that professional competence is in place.
3. Keep checking feedback.
4. Use procedures and formats to make things simpler.
5. Make systems as user friendly as possible.

GETTING PEOPLE THINKING

In organizations which have been heavily proceduralized or where tasks have been numbingly repetitious, the failure of staff to think has come to be recognized as a serious problem.

In the Lancashire mills there used to be a saying that poked fun at office workers as they appeared on the factory floor to ask questions or to chase down answers: 'He's hung his brain up with his hat this morning.' Because the questions that office staff asked were invariably seen as moronic by the shop-floor workers, the belief grew that office workers did not think before asking their questions.

This phenomenon of lack of thought can be associated with the division of labour into separate skills, with the result that individual workers see progressively less of the finished product. Multi-skilling of staff attempts to remove the barriers between roles so that workers must correctly complete each part of the work before progressing. Consequently, they are forced into thinking whether their performance is satisfactory.

Many examples can be cited to show that staff fail to think in their normal routine work, especially in the finance function. Examples include:

- [ ] Debit items on the purchase ledger, outstanding for over three months.
- [ ] When correcting errors, debiting instead of crediting.
- [ ] Cross balances in reports going unchecked.
- [ ] Producing financial accounts that differ from management accounts.
- [ ] Failing to formalize accruals, month after month.
- [ ] Accruing costs to provide results in line with budget.

All of these are common problems that have frequently come to be accepted forms of failure in many companies. Thinking staff would identify these issues at an early stage and empowered staff would take action to avoid the problems arising from them.

18: TO HELP STAFF TO THINK

- [ ] Provide a framework to approach new problems
- [ ] Teach people how to use the framework and think
- [ ] Plan the thinking process
- [ ] Give staff time and freedom to think
- [ ] Help staff to think in teams
- [ ] Allow thinking to become a normal part of daily expectations
- [ ] Allow an initial margin of error
- [ ] Encourage new learning
- [ ] Reinforce beneficial learning

STARTING THE CHANGES — ENERGY PLANT BUILD AND MANAGEMENT COMPANY

Background

This UK subsidiary of a large American company is an engineering and construction contractor for large contracts. The work is largely project based. Engineers design to client specifications, purchase materials, and may then manage the various stages of construction. Providing both staff and clients with timely, relevant and useful information concerning projects is crucial to the success of the company.

Point of view: Group financial director

People make contracts work. Working contracts is our business. We have been very pleased with how quality initiatives have helped the smooth running and better operation of many of the projects that we operate. The way in which our teams now work is a major selling point in new bids.

The relationship with the customer used to be adversarial and often involved pushing one another to the brink. Now, team building is more important and the ability to work together to achieve common goals is essential. Problems are advertised and resolved, rather than hidden away to fester and grow. Fewer arguments result in the faster and better completion of work, and the customer is much more satisfied with the result.

In a large company, many of the staff do not really know where they fit into the organization and how important they really are. The quality environment addresses this issue, and people communicate and learn.

The rules in finance are the same as for the rest of the organization. A few years ago, the attitude was 'Don't tell the staff anything in case you accidentally tell them something confidential'. Now many of these barriers have been broken down by simply showing that the company trusts its staff, and communication is made much easier.

The tactics we employed to drive quality through the organization was to mandate a series of committees:

☐ Quality council: the board.
☐ Quality action committee: composed of divisional directors, setting the pace. This group drives through problem-solving solutions.
☐ Quality action teams: line managers responsible for getting things to work quicker and better.
☐ Quality circles: usually voluntary, which agree on method of implementation.

Unless quality is nurtured and cared for, it is likely to die on the vine. The initiative has to overcome two major obstacles:

1. Management disbelief that staff will start to think about their work.
2. Staff cynicism concerning management willingness to allow the staff to think.

We went to great pains to try and overcome these problems

First a series of meetings was initiated, simply communicating messages to senior staff. They were asked to use similar briefings to update their own staff. We had to really pressure some individuals to start the communication process. A two-day conference addressing some of the big issues really helped — a facilitator was employed to help us cut through the politics, and find out what the issues were.

One of the greatest difficulties is the amount of time that it takes for people to start to change their attitudes. The process will take many years to complete and keeping up the momentum is very difficult. Staff sometimes expect results too soon and they need to understand that it took 30 years to get to this stage. Change will take many months.

Guidelines

1. Structure your approach to implementing quality.
2. Don't try to change the world in a day.
3. Identify the customers — internal and external.
4. Use a catalyst to help change the way you work.
5. Allow contribution from any source.
6. Challenge laziness — disguised as reasons why not.
7. Improve the environment for things to happen.

Useful tips

Most organizations will find the idea of changing their attitudes exceptionally difficult without a very good reason. These reasons can be emphasized if necessary. Make sure that the persons that espouse quality are credible. Claims must be credible and backed by sensible numbers and statistics.

Train staff, and then allow and encourage them to use their new skills in practice.

Writing procedures for an organization is a skill for which an outsider should not be used. The procedure writer needs to understand the accounting systems and the culture.

Laziness is a word that is often avoided because of its connotations of incompetence. But many people avoid change simply because of laziness, tinged with fear of the unknown. Ask not what the company is doing, what are you doing?

BUILDING UP MOMENTUM

To overcome the occasional neglect and inevitable set-backs that are a part of a quality initiative, momentum must be built up and must become part of the culture of the organization. The underlying rule of quality implementation is that success generates success, which generates an expectation of success.

Within quality programmes, one success is likely to lead to another success (in a similar field) because people learn from their experiences. Staff are often surprised how easily quality attitudes can be adopted and how easily they can produce measurable benefits early in a programme. As modest success is achieved, the confidence and motivation of the staff increases, and the organization learns how to implement increasingly complex change successfully.

Once a high level of quality performance has been achieved, it must not be allowed to falter. True quality of performance will only exist in an environment in which it is nurtured and encouraged. It is like a growing plant: unless it is fed and watered, it will wither and die. For the quality programme action and communication is the same as food and water for the plant. If the organization is to see any benefit, the quality programme must be continually fed and watered in the same way as a growing plant.

Converting words and ideals into action requires people who can champion the cause of improvement and who are predisposed to driving the organization forward, regardless of set-backs. Champions are needed for all projects — large and small — and are especially important if substantial effort is required over a long time-span. They set the milestones, and define the targets and objectives, and their powers of persuasion are crucial in achieving the objectives and solving the problems that occur.

Good communication within the organization builds enthusiasm and reinforces the messages of success and how it was achieved. Communicating the message must become a routine way of teaching the organization how to continue improving. The attention span of most organizations is quite short — about three to five weeks — so continuous updating of relevant information is important. Through the organization's communication channels, new reasons for continuing and increasing the pace of change can be disseminated, and announcements made about prizes, awards and recognition of practical achievement.

19: COMMUNICATE SUCCESS

☐ Set modest targets at first
☐ Publicize achievement
☐ Demonstrate how improvement was actually made
☐ Use all of the communication channels:

Personal — face-to-face

—open forum meetings
—grapevine
—team briefings
—action meetings
—quality review meetings

Impersonal — written

—newsletters, papers, magazines
—notice boards
—videos

External

—advertising achievement to staff and to customers
—public relations articles and coverage

IMPROVEMENT AND CHANGE — MOTOROLA CODEX

Background

Motorola Codex is the UK subsidiary of the global company Motorola, set up to provide complete data and voice networking solutions to clients.

Employing approximately 150 people in the UK, the company is profitable and is actively engaged in continuous improvement both operationally and in finance.

Point of view: Director of finance and operations

The reason for the existence of finance is to convert data into information, and information into meaningful business knowledge which is then used to further improve the business.

Quality is about processes and reducing cycle time — by either wiping out the process or making it happen faster. Quality is only part of an overall improvement strategy.

Within a couple of years we have reduced the period taken to prepare accounts from 28 days to 4 and we have managed a simultaneous staff reduction of 35 per cent.

The systems we use are important to this achievement: we adopted a strategy which meant that we purchased the best fully-integrated package available. This enabled some important steps forward to be made:

- ☐ Information now emanates from a single source.
- ☐ We avoid dependence on in-house computer experts.
- ☐ There is no need for accountants to consolidate figures.
- ☐ Many mundane accounting processes are fully automated.

Fully-integrated packages may not give the best functionality, but they still cover almost all one's needs with a minimum of fuss and the minimum of staff.

If it moves and if it is important, we measure it — the achievement of deadlines; the ratio of credit notes to sales invoices (and the reasons for it); the occurrence of errors in numbers; wanted dates against promised dates.

Unless the organization measures, it cannot decide what to improve or the order of priority. Measurement is central to the achievement of quality and continuous improvement.

In striving for continual improvement, we operate to a formula:

- ☐ Provide all levels of staff with problem-solving tools.
- ☐ Set up teams to suggest and make improvements.
- ☐ Help the teams with external facilitation.
- ☐ Keep on and on and on and on.
- ☐ Use process flow charts — simple 'Post-it' notes may suffice.
- ☐ Re-engineer the business processes.
- ☐ Empower the staff to do something positive.

We believe that it is important for the 'background noise' of business to be sifted out of reporting, and this is where financial expertise is really needed. Financial people do not just use numbers — numbers are only the starting point.

To recognize how well you are doing, review benchmarks with colleagues. Internal benchmarking can be beneficial, but it needs to be done externally and internationally to really see the scale of improvement required.

Guidelines

1. Examine your processes, reduce the cycle time persistently.
2. Allow no 'sacred cows'. Allow change to anything.
3. Set very high personal standards.
4. Positively measure achievement.
5. Never stop the improvement process.
6. Set relevant and realistic targets.
7. Empower staff to act.

Pitfalls

Standards and procedures as reflected in BS 5750 and ISO 9000 have an undeserved image of quality. Once the organization has genuinely understood quality, these standards are so low as to be meaningless.

Good management of the teams tasked to achieve continuous improvement in the early days is crucial. Success is important, no matter how small — even if it is just a case of moving the desks around.

CONTINUOUS IMPROVEMENT

Within the action teams, the cycle of improvement — from concept, evolution and development to creation and feedback — must be improved and refined. The tools that are used to assess problems and agree action need to be updated from time to time. As performance improves, the measurement criteria used to monitor performance may need to be changed.

As momentum gathers, the organization will search out ideas and opportunities for change so that prioritized programmes can be implemented. Priorities will be set by making constant reference to the objectives and targets of the organization: it is important that progress takes place in the desired direction. Post-implementation confirmation must be sought to ensure that improvement has brought real and not illusory benefits.

Financially, many organizations approach change with a two-point strategy:

☐ Make immediate savings funded from revenue (profit and loss).
☐ From revenue savings, develop the long-term plan.

By identifying expenses and prioritizing benefits correctly, the organization is able to generate internal funds to support longer-term initiatives. In this way the whole cost of the programme becomes self-funding within a very few months.

However, organizations occasionally have to address and resolve core issues such as culture, structure and central systems. To generate ideas for change and to provide extra impetus, the central pillars of the establishment may need to be replaced. This can range from moving offices or buildings to moving staff into different roles. Within the finance function examples of such large issues include:

☐ scrapping the budgeting process;
☐ scrapping the medium-range planning system;
☐ introducing three-, four- or six-monthly planning cycles;
☐ devolving capital expenditure decisions to local management;
☐ removing all of the accounts payable section — auto payment on GRN;
☐ Sub-contracting out computer information services.

The hype surrounding a large initiative can last for years, if success is emphasized and communication is well managed. Continuing programmes need new vigour to be injected approximately every six to nine months. Even with this degree of resource, converting the more cynical members of staff to quality attitudes is likely to take a few years more.

Taking measurements to identify the pace of change is important in order to confirm that improvement initiatives have not slowed. Routine reporting should therefore include:

- [ ] new inititiatives started;
- [ ] old inititiatives completed;
- [ ] milestones met;
- [ ] milestones missed.

Analyzing trends and using statistical process control within the programme itself will show where more resource or effort should be placed to maintain continuous improvement.

The number of action teams used to plan and implement change affects the speed and number of improvements possible. If team members are too junior or are not empowered to take decisions, team meetings become 'wishing wells' where everything is suggested but nothing is done. If the teams consist of only senior management, junior staff fail to understand the issues and do not take ownership of the problems and their resolution. The composition of action teams must be such that each team is allowed sufficient freedom to make practical change; their terms of reference must not be so wide as to give them an impossible task.

20: BUILDING AND CONTINUING THE IMPROVEMENT

- [ ] Develop and grow champions and sponsors
- [ ] Keep champions motivated
- [ ] Keep teaching permanent staff and updating their knowledge
- [ ] Develop courses so that new employees can achieve quality performance quickly
- [ ] Vary work tasks to maintain interest
- [ ] Encourage people to re-think processes continuously
- [ ] Keep using quality tools to create change
- [ ] Keep successes happening
- [ ] Give prizes
- [ ] Enter competitions for quality
- [ ] Change the underlying assumptions occasionally
- [ ] Join with similar organizations to swap information and compare
- [ ] Benchmark standards internationally
- [ ] Use external facilitators to create extra sparkle
- [ ] Keep team objectives achievable
- [ ] Allow freedom of action
- [ ] Short-term plan — immediate payback
- [ ] Long-term plan — funded from the short-term plan

KEEP THE QUESTIONS COMING — AMERADA HESS LTD

Background

UK turnover £422m. Profitable.

Amerada Hess is the UK subsidiary of a US corporation. It is primarily engaged in the exploration, development, operation and management of oil and gas fields in the North Sea. In addition to four operational business units, there are two services business units. The operational business units have small financial sections responsible for meeting the needs and obligations of the unit, and reporting results to central finance. Central finance is responsible for reporting to the parent, internal corporate reporting, maintenance of corporate standards and controls, and providing services which cannot be efficiently dispersed to business units.

Corporate accounting is responsible for management reporting, capital expenditure forecasting, expenditure authorization control, and accounting for overheads and payables.

Point of view: Corporate Accounting Manager

By continually asking 'Why?' we ensure that adequate control is maintained with an appropriate level of bureaucracy and flexibility. As a company we take a very progressive attitude towards quality in that staff are encouraged to question why they do their jobs and to find simpler ways of achieving the same results.

The company has grown very quickly since becoming an operator rather than just an investing partner. Consequently we did not have the history of some of our competitors and, having learned from the mistakes of others, we could establish new systems and procedures. To maintain the competitive edge, continual improvement is essential — the company is installing a new general ledger system which will significantly improve the flexibility and quality of our data handling and reporting.

Amerada Hess uses tight budgetary/expenditure controls to empower business units, while at the same time ensuring that the company is aware of and approves of change in activity. This requires the maintenance of accurate data and regular and effective cost control against budget. Budgetary transfers are approved corporately. Cost centre managers are responsible for budgets on a 'first spend' basis, under which the total expenditure is controlled and not the net amount.

The company operates a technique that we call 'stewardship', in which individuals or groups take responsibility for a complete asset. They make sure that the whole product (including finance, functionality and time-scale) are to our specification.

Although we have grown rapidly and continually review the overall level and abilities of staff, we use short-term sub-contractors to meet peak work loads or to conduct certain special projects. Growing staff with the organization through training, coaching and opportunity is rewarding for both the staff and the company.

Useful tips

1. Employ employees with the required skills.
2. Encourage employees to think. Ideas generate improvement.
3. Empower staff to make positive improvements.
4. Control costs by using a 'first spend' budget — not net costs after allocations outwards.
5. Keep few staff, as inefficiency can easily result from large departments.

Finance as a function will never disappear. People with financial expertise will always be required for various reasons, including:

☐ ensuring that the right message is interpreted from the figures;
☐ ensuring that local management receive better information;
☐ translating for staff skilled in other disciplines;
☐ ensuring compliance with guidelines and consistency between units.

TRIPS AND TRAPS

Problems will inevitably arise in the course of a quality initiative. Here is some advice on avoiding the most common problems.

Don't start too big

The chances of an organization achieving *total* success in a quality initiative are reckoned to be very small — substantially less than 20 per cent and probably nearer to 0.2 per cent. On the other hand, total failure is also very unlikely.

Keeping early projects relatively small, with a defined brief and realizable objectives, will lead to practical success, which, in turn, will generate expectations of success. When staff have learned team work and can compromise in order to optimize, bigger projects should be attempted.

In the beginning

The following are to be avoided:

☐ an undefined or poorly specified project and benefits;
☐ having no project champion or sponsor;
☐ continuing without top management commitment;
☐ inadequate planning;
☐ insufficient time;
☐ Inadequate resources.

Meeting the needs

In cases where projects are adequately resourced and planned, poor management can still lead to significant problems, such as:

☐ changing objectives part way through the project;
☐ dramatic environment changes (eg major organizational structure changes);

☐   flaws in specifications of measurements and requirements;
☐   timing overlaps and unexpected delays.

Matching provision to need

The root cause of many problems often stems from failing to match provision with need, eg from failing to match:

☐   leadership style with organizational state;
☐   previous experience, skill, and knowledge with the given task;
☐   the extent of empowerment with employee ability.

Failure

The main reasons for programme failure are:

1.   Management ego

Many senior managers have not yet been converted to the vision of quality, even though they make speeches as if they have. They seek the prestige that an award might bestow, and the opportunity to use the kite-mark on their paperwork.

Such individuals say the right words but fail to act in the right way.

2.   Accountants

A remarkable number of financial specialists fail to see the need for quality in service organizations, and especially within the finance function. Accountants are the largest single group cited for causing the failure of quality initiatives.

3.   Cynicism and disbelief

In established organizations that have no history of change and empowerment, staff are reluctant to believe that management will actually start to trust employees to perform their tasks properly.

Employees can usually cite several other management initiatives that failed to achieve their objectives. Staff need positive signs and genuine action.

4.   Loss of commitment

Staff turnover or promotion within the company can cause crucial champions to be lost to the project. Expertise built up over months and years can easily be lost if insufficient attention is paid to succession planning.

5.   Lack of success

From trying to do too much, too quickly.

6. 'It costs too much'

Numerous managers declare that they are unable to spend pennies to gain extra pounds. Taking the incremental approach is essential in these instances.

7. 'It takes too long'

Poorly prioritized projects which create long periods with little progress generate complaints of delay and time-wasting.

8. Apathy

From years of neglect, mistrust and suspicion some staff may need more than promises to start believing again in management abilities.

9. Laziness

For staff and managers who have grown used to an inefficient way of working, improving performance at work appears to be more difficult than doing nothing.

10. Stupidity

When managers prefer to play politics rather than improve overall performance, results invariably suffer.

11

A Glance at the Future

DEVELOPMENTS IN FINANCIAL INFORMATION

Financial accounting

As world money markets extend their hold and influence over corporations and governments seeking access to substantial funds, the suppliers of finance are likely to increase their requirements for information. If this trend continues to develop organizations could be required to publish:

☐ quarterly or monthly bulletins;
☐ detailed information on sales, locations, product mix, margins, etc;
☐ transparent accounts — where all off balance sheet items are visible and all formats are prescribed by regulatory authorities.

Though many finance directors may perform to the above specification already, there is no official requirement to do so. In recent years the development of accounting standards and exposure drafts has improved the general degree of managerial and professional understanding of financial accounts. Whether the general public or commercial management have gained anything from the huge expense incurred is open to debate. On an international scale, UK company reporting is increasingly emulating the reporting requirements of the US, due in part to the fact that numerous British companies now raise finance in overseas markets.

As European financial markets grow and develop, they will introduce greater reporting restrictions on their domestic companies and require additional information. The result of the demand for greater information will be increasing pressure for finance functions of all types to use:

☐ more automation;
☐ better information systems;
☐ fewer people.

The only approach that can achieve this, and simultaneously

lead to the improvement of decision-making within the organization, is that of quality.

Management accounting

Management accounts are not subject to the same degree of public scrutiny as published financial accounts, and accountancy bodies and institutes have not developed international management accounting guidelines. As a result, finance professionals have been able to meet user needs with great flexibility, being unconstrained by narrowly defined statements and procedures.

In recent years the level of interest in management accounting has greatly increased. Management have realized that by using accounting information intelligently, decisions can be improved to affect positively the fortunes of the organization. The profession of management accounting has thrived; many companies now prefer to recruit management rather than chartered accountants.

The range of information contained in management accounts has been widening year by year. There has been a move away from prescriptive financial accounting towards decentralization and personalized service. Management accounting can accommodate many different treatments of underlying facts, which results in internal reports being user specific and non-standard. Multi-dimensions within data and the ability to manipulate variables in reports have made the new approaches essential to users.

In turn, the flexibility of new, non-standard data has led to increasing levels of irritation with older, more prescribed management accounting methods and systems. At the heart of the dissatisfaction lies the fact that routine information does not show what the user wants to know. Accountants are needed to interpret the meaning of the numbers, and financial complexity hides operational simplicity. The users are line managers who want to make decisions based on clear and unambiguous data. Costing systems that were conceptualized during the late 19th and early 20th centuries, and developed over the last 50 years, have fallen into disrepute. We will now look briefly at the reasons for this.

Standard costing

The cost of an item is less relevant than the cost of a process because the process cost is a function of time and the item cost is a function of allocation. There is an assumed homogeneity of output which is false — modern products are similar, but each one can be different.

Knowing the fully apportioned overhead cost of an item does

206 / Quality in the Finance Function

not help managers to make decisions concerning the process. Amortizing sunk costs bewilders decision-makers and obscures what would otherwise be simple decisions.

Standards hide potential for improvement. For example, if the standard says four are needed, there is no incentive to get adequate performance from three.

Marginal costing

Basing decisions on the extra costs incurred by producing one extra unit can lead to strange effects — product pricing, capital investment or production priorities.

The fixed costs ignored in the calculation of marginal cost cause major difficulties when new plant must be funded from profits.

Contribution analysis

Arguments about whether costs are fixed or variable have made decisions based on this kind of analysis subject more to opinion than to fact. Only where cash is the prime motive for business and capital expenditure is severely restricted is this now a recognized 'best method'.

Easier access to huge volumes of data has simplified the task of designing and improving information and new approaches to old problems have been developed. One of these developments was activity based costing (ABC).

Activity based costing

Activity based costing was recognized during the 1980s as being a viable and beneficial way of reviewing and reporting the costs of an organization. This was a dramatic step forward for the accountancy profession. By using ABC organizations have gradually come to recognize that knowing how much an item costs is of little value. The significance to the business of understanding cost is in knowing how much cost was added in order to generate total customer added value. In using ABC, the primary task of finance is to identify whether costs should have been incurred and whether those costs could be reduced, minimized or avoided.

The method involves collecting costs associated with the *causes* of the expenditure. These are called 'cost drivers'. The 'drivers' for a credit control department may frequently be the total number of sales invoices processed, whereas the 'drivers' for the accounts payable could be the total number of lines ordering goods and services from suppliers. To help managers identify the drivers of their business, processes must be dissected and the underlying reasons understood as to why a task is performed. Collecting costs in this way can result in the dismantling of function-focused departments and their reconstruction as process-focused. The principles of ABC are very similar to the identification of costs of quality as discussed in Chapter 7.

Examples of cost drivers include:

- material movements;
- part numbers;
- parts received in the month;
- products manufactured;
- options on the products;
- changes to planning schedules;
- suppliers;
- units scrapped;
- engineering changes;
- process changes;
- number of employees.

ABC has helped many companies to translate supply-oriented information — where data gathered relates only to the costs incurred — into demand-oriented information.

The change to an ABC accounting system tends to lead to a reduction in the types of cost that are collected. Frequently only two types of cost are collected:

1. direct materials;
2. conversion costs.

Activity based costing also affects companies which use advanced manufacturing techniques, such as just in time. Cost drivers are often derived from analysis of the demand systems that pull products through the manufacturing process.

Forecasting

As more information about financial transactions and their implications becomes available, the data can be used to attempt to predict events in the future with greater accuracy. Advanced computer models are available that can use the statistics of a process to assess the impact of changes made in the fundamental assumptions. Simple spreadsheet packages have advanced to facilitate massive 'what-if' calculations that can test the outcomes of many different decisions. Sensitivity analysis has become a much simpler task. Laptop computers can be plugged into computer networks and small, portable printers mean that users can have access to data wherever they happen to work.

Computers have revolutionized budgeting and planning through the introduction of multi-dimensional spreadsheets. In addition to speeding up the calculation processes, these systems facilitate simple consolidations of many subsets of data. As the manipulation and presentation of data becomes increasingly automated, the third ingredient for success can receive more attention, ie the development of intellect.

Data collection

Companies and organizations are beginning to recognize that data and information can increase in value if it is shared. If organizations can overcome the lack of trust normally found in supplier/customer relationships, sales data can be used to provide great benefits to all parties.

Where the sharing of detailed sales information is the basis of the relationship between supplier and customer, computer technology has made possible the avoidance of processing suppliers' sales invoices, purchase orders and goods received notes. In such circumstances the parties are customer oriented, which gives them the opportunity to be more demand responsive.

In coming years, the trend toward paperless trading will increase, as will reliance on computing power. Optical discs and similar new technology means that the power and influence of computers will continue to grow, and will be more accessible to users. Cable networks and telephone and satellite development will result in the ability to link computers seamlessly together, and the creation of more easily accessible data.

Very advanced technology is very expensive, so only the most forward-thinking companies will be at the leading edge of development. Until the new technology is available, and cheap enough for the majority of organizations to adopt new approaches, incremental changes to data collection methods will occur. Examples of some of the steps include:

□ Bar code reading — computers recognize names and numbers.
□ Optical character recognition (OCR) — computers read printed documents.
□ Remote unit ordering — sales data collected in hand-held units and telephoned through direct to the computer.
□ Voice recognition — computers listen to and understand verbal instructions from humans.
□ Single stock systems — held by retailer, wholesaler and manufacturer.
□ Customer needs' estimates, based on previous purchase history.

Under pressure to reduce inventories, increase margins and improve returns on assets, data collection must become wholly automatic and customer driven. Point of sale information will therefore grow in importance and will affect all industry processing, not just retail. Suppliers of services and products will be wedded to computer systems which record customer purchases and new needs.

For the finance function, this has incredible implications. Computers will gradually assume the role of instructor and shrinking numbers of employees will merely check the output.

Human intervention will only be required when errors are made or the environment changes. This scenario has already become a reality for a significant proportion of the dealing in stocks and shares and financial instruments.

DEVELOPMENTS IN FINANCIAL SERVICES

From the business angle

As new software is developed, the automation of manual tasks will continue. Some tasks will disappear as processes are re-engineered to avoid the work.

Through business process re-engineering (BPR), purchase invoices and goods received notes could disappear, and for many organizations so could sales invoices. As more supplier relationships come to rely on direct debits to bank accounts, credit control staffing will decline to minimal levels.

A number of major banks embarked on test-bed BPR in 1993. This is expected to result in dramatic manpower reductions before the turn of the century. Building societies, insurance companies, pension fund managers, trust funds and brokers are all likely to follow suit within a few years.

As technology develops, new markets will be cultivated so that new added value can be generated. Financial engineering (ie the use of financial instruments to release capital) will further develop to help organizations utilize their assets better. Computerized trading will extend its dominance of the financial markets. Fewer individuals will be involved in bigger commodity deals.

Financial experts will play a crucial role in defining how computers operate, and in ensuring that sufficient, correct data is actually gathered.

The domestic angle

Data collected at the point of sale will provide the customer-oriented information demanded by all users in the supply chain. Targeted and detailed information will enable the supplier of the products and services to anticipate customer needs and preferences in order to provide an improved match between service and need. Information collected at these points includes credit card and payment details, as well as the physical items or services and their value.

The immediate knowledge of sales details will facilitate better instructions to suppliers and make stock holding reductions possible. Analysis of the data can also result in the identification of more sales opportunities for the supplier. This marketing influence will increase the rate of growth in home purchasing, or direct telephone sales. The success of this new approach to selling financial services is apparent from the achievements of First Direct Bank and the Royal Bank of Scotland's Direct Line Insurance services.

The increased benefits to customers of buying products and services from non-retail points of sale may lead more people to set up a bank account to take advantage of the new possibilities.

Vanishing jobs, and new roles

Automation of manual processes will lead to organizations requiring fewer administrative staff in total, and those who remain will have broad-based, highly developed skills. Gradually, users of information will learn financial skills and become increasingly adept at manipulating and applying data and the resulting information for themselves. The transition from specialist functions to multi-functional competences will take many years.

Those organizations which embark on this path will be able to manage the transfer of information successfully, and they will grasp and take advantage of new opportunities as they are presented. The staff involved in the transition will be faced with the choice of changing and growing into new roles or stagnating. Organizations which fail to change will be left behind as their competitors make dramatic improvements and rapidly gain market share.

Lower-level, single-skill personnel are more likely to be made redundant as working practices are re-engineered and replacement systems are installed. Opportunities will be created to transfer across to productive roles where new skills can be taught and old skills used to supplement the quality improvement process. Many organizations which adopt quality employ the same number of staff as they did before, but multi-skilling is now required. Training and education to gain new skills and abilities is the way forward for individuals.

For senior providers of financial services a much broader education in other disciplines will come to be an essential prerequisite. The breadth of understanding of other disciplines will add value for employers — many companies now require an MBA or postgraduate degree in addition to a financial qualification before promotion to senior ranks. General management will appreciate financial information and advice that adequately encompasses marketing, operations and delivery considerations.

Due to the reducing requirement for junior staff, great pressure will be brought to bear on the number of senior posts. Ultimately, cost pressures will lead to many specialist financial roles being sub-contracted out so that the organization can maintain a balance between permanent junior and senior staff and available external skills.

WORLD CLASS FINANCIAL INFORMATION AND FINANCIAL SERVICES

For a department or function to be world class demands a number of measures. World class manufacturers and service organizations are those that compare favourably with any competitor internationally on a range of financial and non-financial criteria. The objective of being world class is to survive the longest by being the best — this is not necessarily by also being the cheapest. The term world class usually refers to the degree of efficiency with which an item of output is produced.

For the finance function, world class indicators have not yet been set for either information or service providers. Organizations should realize that employing the best financial systems and staff in order to beat rivals on both quality and cost criteria is no longer sufficient. A broader range of services and faster responses are necessary to sustain and increase competitive advantage.

Currently, two opposing views are being aired:

1. Finance is an integral part of the business whose function is to assist and further satisfy customer demands in whatever ways are possible and sensible.
2. Finance exists only to maximize the discounted value of future cash flows from evaluated projects.

A world class finance function must be able to reconcile these views satisfactorily and demonstrate that maximum service as in 1) can be provided within the financial constraints of 2). Being able to prove whether the organization meets world class criteria can be approached as follows:

☐ Achievement of business objectives — requiring some interpretation of statements and statistics.
☐ Achievement of financial objectives — requiring comparison of actuals to forecasts, with hindsight.
☐ Underlying comparative advantage — demanding detailed analysis of national and international performance.
☐ Dissection and evaluation of each process within the finance function.
☐ Published accounts — normal financial ratio analysis.

When comparing internationally, performance within one-year periods is far less relevant than the trend of performance. Consequently, criteria can be defined and measurements taken in each of the categories above. Some of the criteria will be financial, some statistical and some opinion:

☐ **Business objectives**
— market growth and market maturity;
— market share;

- intensity of competition;
- price leadership;
- investment leadership;
- customer quality leadership;
- environmental effects of dramatic change;
- orientation of financial to non-financial priorities.

☐ **Financial objectives**
- reliability of underlying data;
- credibility of information and/or services provided;
- stakeholder valuation of organization;
- customer/consumer valuation of organization;
- supplier/staff valuation of organization;
- development of staff internally.

☐ **Comparative advantage**
- degree of financial improvement sought (annually);
- degree of financial improvement achieved;
- statistical measures of user utility of services;
- effect of different levels of training and education.

☐ **Dissection of finance function processes**
- compared costs of comparable services;
- measure of the use of information technology;
- service effectiveness measures;
- speed of response.

☐ **Published accounts**
- ratio analysis;
- working capital analysis;
- asset investment income stream analysis;
- sensitivity statistics.

Some recent work by Coopers & Lybrand consultancy staff has begun the discussion concerning the definition of world class accounting. It remains to be seen whether their approach will be taken up by industry leaders.

WORLD CLASS ACCOUNTING — BOC

Background

BOC is a multinational and approaches solutions globally where possible and sensible. Quality plays a central role in every operating company and lies at the heart of financial thinking in the head office at Windlesham.

International experience is used to teach others how to benefit from adopting the quality approach. By exchanging experiences, the process is both legitimized and developed, which leads to substantial benefits for the group.

The amount of data given to the board has decreased by 75 per cent in the last two years. This has been achieved by cutting out unnecessary or irrelevant facts and statistics. Speedy knowledge transfer is the objective of the reporting system, which uses picture book approaches and other innovative methods.

Point of view: Group controller

The four main functions of finance that we recognize and try to measure are:

1. processing;
2. control;
3. decision support;
4. financial leadership.

Working within the strategy outlined earlier, the company is successfully progressing in all four functions.

Processing Staff analyze errors, and attend to causal problems in the system. We obliterate duplication and automate work so that data is gathered and processed once only. Facilities are shared where economies can be made; global telecommunications networks have made 'centres of excellence', in which specialist skills are grouped in particular locations, an option. For instance, a number of sites share sales ledger functions.

Control By changing the attitudes and beliefs of the staff, wholesale changes to financial control become possible. When credit control staff ask 'How can we help you pay this debt?' responses are much more positive. Control has to take on a new meaning in which the customers' needs are crucial.

When resolving problems, one has to treat the disease, not the symptoms. Pressure on overhead costs can mean that within financial decision-making, we seriously consider the idea of trading audit cost against business risk. This kind of philosophy of risk identification and assessment has to start at the top. By empowering more staff to perform properly in their role, directors can concentrate on higher strategic issues, where they can add value for the company.

Decision support Managerial skills and the associated numeracy skills are important characteristics of finance staff. Finance must help to run the business by creating the right environment for decisions. Such things as systems improvements, asking fundamental questions and continually improving processes are crucial to future success.

Financial leadership The benchmarking of our major products and processes and the taking of appropriate action will result in the group continuing to be a world leader for its products. We intend that such leadership will also exist in our finance function.

Leadership attitudes have developed quality to the point where there is an argument that budgets should be radically reviewed because they lock improvements into a 12-month time-frame. To avoid annual budgets becoming an unnecessary constraint to continuous improvement, we are moving to a rolling forecast with emphasis on a three-month cycle.

There are many other aspects to the achievement of quality within the group. Perhaps the more important ones are:

Training By taking time with individuals, they will gain the rounded business knowledge that will be required as they rise in seniority. For trainee accountants, we operate a six-monthly change of responsibility in a three-year programme.

Personal characteristics As a company we embody the cultural differences of America, Britain and Japan. We are looking to embrace the best of these abilities in finance.

Champions The QiP needs champions to ensure that the targets are reached on time, within budget, first time. Consequently the quality programmes involve as many champions as possible.

TAKE A POSITIVE ATTITUDE

Organizations which make and sell products have been demanding faster turn-rounds, quicker development times for new products and more detailed information from external suppliers. Simultaneously, a better quality of both product and service has been stipulated and price reductions have been required. A similar process of change has affected those who provide public services, the main difference being that the driving force for change is the charter which describes the minimum standards that should be provided.

In the same way as buyers of products and users of services, finance function users are becoming more demanding. Financial services must be matched to personal needs, and it must be fast, effective and cheap. Financial information users want to understand the causes of relationships between data, and they want to be able to recognize and modify underlying assumptions. Much greater access to data is required to allow more extensive evaluations of actual and potential decisions. Frequently, access and information are required that will enable users not to have to make any future demands for information and so be able to make their future decisions unaided.

At the core of good financial functions lies intelligent questioning and thinking responses. To elicit the best responses, personal attitudes are crucial:

1. Negative attitudes lead to individualism and poor decisions:
   — Finance stands as the judge of others and frequently acts as the decision-maker, especially where large sums or capital expenditure is involved.
   — The suggestions of others are evaluated only in financial terms. Non-financial considerations are frequently completely ignored.
   — Few options are considered when making decisions, and modifications to basic assumptions from non-finance personnel are actively discouraged.
2. Positive attitudes lead to team work and performance improvement:

— Specialists work with colleagues to develop and evaluate suggestions. Value for the user is increased as more options and other considerations are included in the discussions. Balanced arguments are pursued, frequently based on learning from previous completed projects.

A negative attitude is much easier to adopt than a positive one and it is easier to criticize than to make positive and constructive comment. Criticism hides apathy and apathy hides laziness. Criticism demotivates and lowers morale. Even when justified, criticism has never been known to add value.

To keep up with changes in developing markets, a challenging and positive attitude must be maintained. Though this will mean a fundamental behavioural change for many involved in finance, change is essential in order to fulfil the potential of modern technology and to add value for users and decision-makers.

Appendix

Statutes

1844   Joint Stock Companies Act
1882   Bills of Exchange Act
1889   Factors Act
1890   Partnership Act
1925   Law of Property Act
1929   Finance Act
1948   Companies Act
1956   Restrictive Trade Practices Act
1960   Charities Act
1961   Factories Act
1965   Hire Purchase Act
1967   Misrepresentation Act
1968   Trade Descriptions Act
1969   Employers Liability Act
1971   Unsolicited Goods and Services Act
1972   European Communities Act
1973   Fair Trading Act
1973   Supply of Goods (Implied Terms) Act
1974   Consumer Credit Act
1975   Sex Discrimination Act
1976   Stock Exchange Act
1976   Restrictive Trade Practices Act
1977   Unfair Contract Terms Act
1977   Torts (Interference with Goods) Act
1978   Consumer Safety Act (Amended 1986)
1979   Banking Act
1979   Sale of Goods Act, 1893
1980   Competition Act
1982   Insurance Companies Act
1982   Supply of Goods and Services Act
1984   Data Protection Act
1985   Companies Act
1985   Company Securities (Insider Dealing) Act
1986   Insolvency Act
1986   Building Society Act
1986   Financial Services Act

1987 Banking Act
1987 Consumer Protection Act
1989 Companies Act
1989 Water Act
1989 Employment Acts, 1978, 1980, 1988

Statutory Instruments

1984 Stock Exchange (Listing) Regs
1986 Insolvency Rules
      Companies (Disqualification Orders)
1987 Financial Services (Disclosure of Information)
      Insolvency Rules
      Companies (Mergers)
      Insolvent Companies (Unfit Directors)
1989 Bank (Administration Proceedings)
      Insider Dealing
1990 Overseas Companies (Accounts)
      Companies (Summary of Financial Statements)
      Company Auditors (Examinations) Regulations

European Community

1956 Treaty of Rome
1992 Maastricht Treaty

Bibliography

Books

Archier and Serieyx (1987) *The Type 3 Company*, Gower, Aldershot
British Standards Institution (1991) BS 5750, Part 8, *Quality Systems*
British Standards Institution (1992) BS 6143, Part 1, *Guide to the Economics of Quality*
Broadgate and Savage (1991) *Commercial Law*, Butterworths, London
D'Arcy (1988) *Company Law*, Aina HLT Group
De Bono (1981) *Atlas of Management Thinking*, Mercury, London
Drummond, H (1992) *The Quality Movement*, Kogan Page, London
DTI (1992) *The Case for Costing Quality*, HMSO, Norwich
Ernst & Young Quality Improvement Group (1992) *Total Quality*, Kogan Page, London
Fraser-Robinson, J (1991) *Total Quality Marketing*, Kogan Page, London
Goldratt and Fox (1986) *The Race*, North River Press
Grant and Leavenworth (1980) *Statistical Process Control*, McGraw-Hill, Maidenhead
Hall (1992) *The Quality Manual*, Wiley, Chichester
Hammer and Champy (1993) *Re-engineering the Corporation*, Brearley Publishing, London
Ishikawa, K (1982) *Guide to Quality Control*, Kraus
Johansson, McHugh, Pendlebury and Wheeler (1993) *Business Process Re-engineering*, Wiley, Chichester
Juran and Gyrna (1988) *Juran's Quality Control Handbook*, McGraw-Hill, Maidenhead
Keenan and Riches (1990) *Business Law*, Pitman, London
Lawlor (1985) *Productivity Improvement Manual*, Gower Press, Aldershot
McMillen, N (1991) *Statistical Process Control and Company Wide Improvement*, IFS Ltd
Robinson, (1991) *Continuous Improvements in Operations*, Productivity Press, Mass
Schonberger (1986) World Class Manufacturing, The Free Press, New York
Taguchi (1983) *Introduction to Quality Engineering*, Kraus
Teboul, J (1988) *De-industrialise Service for Quality*, Prentice-Hall, New Jersey
Teboul, J (1991) Managing Quality Dynamics, Prentice Hall, New Jersey
Townsend (1986) *Commit to Quality*, Wiley, Chichester
Walton (1991) *Deming Management at Work*, Mercury, London

Research papers and articles

Clark, F (1992) 'Quality and service: a key focus for performance in the public sector', Research paper, Henley Management College

Hammer, C (1990) 'Re-engineering work: Don't automate, obliterate', Harvard Business Review, August 1990

Horner, R (1990) 'A statistical approach to vendor certification', Research paper, Washington DC University

McFadyen, L (1993) 'World class finance', Management Accounting, September 1993

Rees, JL and Rigby, P (1988) 'Total quality control, the Hewlett Packard way', Research paper, Edinburgh University

Stewart, RH (1992) 'Service quality from disciplined behaviour', Management Accounting, November 1992

Statistics

Eurostat 1981–2: Census of Population, 3C, 2C

Labour Force Statistics, OECD, 1991

Statistical Yearbook, 37th issue, United Nations

Index